Everything I Need to Know About

BUSINESS

I Learned from

Hip-Hop

A MILLENNIAL'S GUIDE TO MAKING BANK

GILES MILLER

Everything I Need to Know About Business I Learned from Hip-Hop: A Millennial's Guide to Making Bank

Copyright © 2017 by Giles Miller. All Rights Reserved.

For information about this title or to order other books and/or electronic media, contact the publisher:
Giles Miller
1899 High Grove Lane
Naperville, IL 60540
hgilesmiller@hotmail.com

ISBN: 978-0-9989209-0-0 (Hardcover)
        978-0-9989209-5-5 (Softcover)
        978-0-9989209-9-3 (eBook)

Printed in the United States of America
Cover and Interior design: 1106 Design

CONTENTS

CONTENTS

HIP-HOP GENESIS:
STARTUP CONSIDERATIONS

Hip-Hop's garish displays of wealth, brassy characters, and rags-to-riches folklore get people juiced. The platinum grills, blinged-out jewelry, candy-colored supercars, designer clothes, and tricked-out homes are exciting and eye catching. The lively and raw personalities of its most prominent figures have appealed to youth culture for generations because of the strength, independence, and possibility they represent. The music itself ranged from deep and tragic with artists like Tupac and Biggie Smalls, to the easy and lightweight like Lil Jon and Ludacris. For all of these reasons and more, Hip-Hop is entertaining showbiz.

However, the business world did not appreciate Hip-Hop for the value it offered. It was too self-absorbed to see past visible differences to the qualities beneath the surface. In fact, other than the unreformed, grinning hippies, Ben Cohen and Jerry Greenfield of Ben and Jerry's Ice Cream, there wasn't much diversity in business, and even that wasn't much. Few successful institutions defied the conservative, buttoned-down image of the mainstream business world. As a result, few people outside of the music industry looked at Hip-Hop as something that had economic lessons to teach. Boy, were those people wrong.

There was professional wisdom sewn into the lyrics, lives, and life lessons of Hip-Hop from its very beginning. If business books bore you, you have an opportunity to learn startup considerations from *The Source* founders Jonathan Shecter and David Mays, sales and marketing from P Diddy, management fundamentals from 50 Cent, human resources from Macklemore, project management from Ice-T, business finance from Queen Latifah, and major changes in business from Dr. Dre.

Hip-Hop will teach you everything you need to know about business. And you thought Hip-Hop was just good music . . .

Hustle Hard: Picking a Business and Staking a Claim

Aubrey "Drake" Graham had it all. He sold millions of albums, captured the attention of tens of millions of fans, and had the love of Hip-Hop's most adorable sandwich-making stagemom. In his song "Unforgettable," Drake introduced us to the one who stole his heart, The Game, also known as "business." It's easy to see how profit-seeking enterprises attracted him. There was something about economic activity that made the Grammy Award winner call business the love of his life. The challenge, excitement, and rewards were enough to convince Drake to start a record label, OVO Sound, and launch his own clothing line. It was intensely creative work for him. It had some of the deep self-expression of art and the intense competitive atmosphere of professional sports. Oh, and there is the opportunity to make piles of cash . . . that probably helps, too.

From commercial fishing to space communication support services, 600,000 businesses start in the U.S. every year. With millions of ways to make a buck, it is hard to see what one new company could possibly have in common with another. The answer is to step back and look again; the similarities start to show up. There are four pillars to starting a successful business: passion, value creation, technical ability, and financing. The presence of each one reinforces the others. Without any one of them, the business is less stable.

An entrepreneur has to want to be on the job, putting in the hours, in good times and bad. A leader's passion can add energy to the workforce and inspire the clientele. It is visible in the devotion to customer service, eagerness for new opportunities, and even the desire to do better when things go wrong. A lack of passion in the leader invites the temptation to quit at the first signs of difficulty. Business is hard, so a leader has to want to be there doing the work and meeting the inevitable challenges. Passion fuels the enterprise at the outset and provides a cushion of resilience to bounce back during the tough times.

Lauryn Hill grew up in the middle-class city of East Orange, New Jersey, about 13 miles west of New York City. Born to a musically inclined family, Lauryn was immersed in entertainment from the beginning, with her mother playing piano and her father singing in nightclubs. With her own natural talent and training, it was no surprise that she would develop a lifelong love for music. After just a few successes performing in public, singing at school basketball games, in choir recitals, and even the late-night classic, *It's Showtime at the Apollo,* Lauryn realized that she could do more with her musical interest than just amateur performances.

Backed by her high school friends, Prakazrel "Pras" Michel and Wyclef Jean, Lauryn formed The Fugees. The three friends spent hours on end together, and in time they mixed musical styles like Reggae, Soul, and Hip-Hop to create their own unique sound. There were few groups of similar quality and drive like The Fugees at the time, which helped the group land a record contract with Columbia and Ruffhouse Records in 1993. The three practiced relentlessly to produce their first album, *Blunted on Reality.* The album flopped commercially, but, despite the setback, Wyclef, Pras, and Lauryn rededicated themselves to create their second album, *The Score*. That album would dominate the charts throughout 1996, earn them a Grammy Award for Best R&B Performance, and sell 6 million albums. However, it wouldn't have happened without their shared loved of the music, desire for success even in the dark times, and commitment to each other. That is passion.

Value creation is about solving problems. The nearly unlimited spectrum of goods and services that business provides to the world gives consumers something they need—from the simple to the complex, from the legal to the super-criminal, and from the highly profitable to the ruinous. All products try to create value. The company has to make or do something that satisfies a customer need at a return greater than the costs to supply it. It is the reason people are willing to part with their cash. Without value creation, an enterprise cannot last.

In entertainment, there are few demographics more attractive than the 12- to 24-year-olds. They are the center cut of the steak, and in the 1980s and '90s, record companies pursued the demographic like horny adolescent males after a Victoria's Secret Angel. The results for the music industry were about as predictably disappointing. Despite their institutional experience selling traditionally Black music like Soul and R&B music, record labels seemed to be at a loss for how to deal with the polyglot Hip-Hop fan base. Internal marketing efforts were hit-and-miss, and even when a Rap album sold well, companies had a hard time understanding what made them successful. Hip-Hop was outside of their experience, and the marketing teams of the major record labels of the time were simply unable to understand how to reach the young fan of the new genre. That was the value proposition that Steve Rifkind stepped in to provide.

His company, SRC, could relieve ham-fisted record labels of the frustrations of marketing the fastest-growing musical genre in entertainment at the time. Rifkind blanketed the means of distribution. He got his songs on the radio stations that played Hip-Hop. He had an "in" at MTV for video promotion. In retail, SRC knew the stores that were selling the most music and were likely to be a sales hub for any hit record. But to be honest, the record labels could and did do a lot of that marketing.

What Rifkind and his team had that the labels didn't was a grassroots, word-of-mouth, tastemaking process using a crew of kids who could influence their friends and others. The street team had a map of locations up and down the West Coast that was sure to get the word out about the products that they were pushing. They would call on record stores, Black radio stations, barbershops, gang hangouts, bars, and nightclubs to push the product that labels hired them to promote.[1] And they did it in a way that seemed genuine and authentic to their customers, who enjoyed hearing hot new sounds before anyone else. That was something that the stuffed shirts at the in-house marketing departments of the record labels couldn't do, and SRC profited by solving their problem and providing that value.

Technical ability is the competence and talent to deliver the value element of the business. It is the ingenious programming of the software designer, the fine craftsmanship of the tradesman, the slick marketing of a social media service, or the indispensability of a lifeguard at an Olympic swimming event. The better a person is at the core tasks of the business, the higher the chances are that customers will appreciate its quality and usefulness. Conversely, failure in technical ability is about the quickest way out of business, since no one wants to pay for shoddy work.

To get out of the Detroit slums, Marshall "Eminem" Mathers worked his ass off to be the best rapper he could be. Eminem and his friends practiced whenever they could get together. They wrote songs, performed for friends, and battled in underground clubs where competition was brutal. Contenders stepped up to hurl insults as quickly and creatively as they could, and the crowd determined the winners by acclamation. The losers were chased off the stage under a hail of insults and laughter. The scenes of these showdowns were captured in his semi-autobiographical movie, *8 Mile*. When Eminem was able to dominate the club scene with his tight rhymes and raw presentation, he had proved that he had the skills to move up to the big leagues with Dr. Dre at Aftermath Entertainment.

Once at Aftermath, Eminem continued to own the Rap game. He released eight studio albums with one double platinum, one triple platinum, three quadruple platinum, and two diamond albums. He won 15 Grammy Awards, and he was the only Hip-Hop artist to win an Academy Award, which he earned for Best Original Song, "Lose Yourself." While success sometimes has a compounding effect, which could account for some of his later sales figures, Eminem would not have gotten anywhere near the stratosphere of success he achieved if he had not worked to become an incredibly good rapper in the first place.

The Wu-Tang Clan was correct when saying that Cash Rules Everything Around Me in their hit "C.R.E.A.M." because money is the lifeblood of a business. Without it, there won't be much activity for very long. Every company requires some kind of cash at startup and during continuing operations whether it is for a store's rent, stocking inventory, buying equipment, paying wages, or entertaining your entourage. Leaders have to know how much money the business needs and how to get it on time. Too many companies that had people with the requisite passion for the work, value-creating products, and the technical abilities to develop a loyal following failed without sufficient funds.

Financing normally comes from business loans from banks or personal loans from friends, family, or investors. The terms of these agreements vary based on the strength of the business plan, the assets and talent it has, the capital required, and the risks or likelihood of success. The better and more manageable they are, the better the financing terms. The worse they are, the more likely it is that the company will have to accept some ugly rates, surrender substantial collateral, or look for a different source of funding.

In the 1980s, most of the action in Hip-Hop was taking place in the East Coast's gritty club scene or the hot, high-octane streets of the West Coast. It was easy to overlook activities in other parts of the country, but the most important empire of the Dirty South got its start in New Orleans at that time. The brothers, Ronald "Slim" and Brian "Birdman" Williams, were sons of local businessman and entrepreneur Johnny Williams. They learned the value of independence and hard work at their father's grocery stores, bars, and laundromat; and, with their love of increasingly popular Rap music, the two decided to start their own label, Cash Money Records.[2]

Initially, Birdman and Slim had a true startup operation. They picked up little-known artists where they could find them locally in bars, clubs, and other hangouts. With no money to throw around, they were recording albums in the kitchen with borrowed equipment.[3] They figured out how to manage their talent, sell their products, and turn a profit—all on a shoestring. While the major record labels fought tooth and nail over what they considered to be the prize of Hip-Hop, dominance of East and West Coast music, the Williams brothers established a significant regional presence throughout the South, which they then looked to expand.

"Of course, once the major record labels heard about these two brothers moving thousands of units in the Big Easy, they all wanted to sign them."[4] Birdman and Slim saw the majors' desire for a deal as a way to get the formal financing that had been so elusive in the past. They insisted that the record company loan them millions on favorable terms as a condition of any deal. That money would then be reinvested to expand Cash Money, allowing it to grow even further. This financing piece was very lucrative for Birdman and Slim. But the fact that Universal Music Group ultimately agreed to leave Cash Money with rights to the master tapes—and charging a pittance for album distribution—ensured that there would be plenty of future-royalty revenue.[5] Holding on to those would be their own form of financing.

Baby and Slim had grown from a small enterprise with no capital into a serious record label with the serious financial backing of an industry heavyweight. The Williams brothers' savvy management, the incredible talent of Cash Money's artists, and the Universal loan all wove together to build the Dirty South's music-industry powerhouse. However, none of it would have been possible without access to cash to keep the company going.

Pursuit of Happiness: Learning the Rules of the Game

Every industry has its own rules. Managers need to understand them to run their businesses. Analyzing the products, customers, sales methods, financing, and competition provides entrepreneurs vital data points to understand on the road to success. The traditional routes to business enlightenment pass through only a few information channels: publications, trade associations, and mentors and social networks. Each has its advantages.

Print media isn't the be-all and end-all information clearinghouse it once was, but it's not dead. Highly specialized publications and general industry periodicals adapted to online and social media environments provide convenient and inexpensive access to information. They offer interesting articles on market trends, supplier advertisements, and intelligence on competitor activities. A Google search will connect you to a cornucopia of audio, video, and text content in fractions of a second, no matter how compartmentalized or obscure. You are limited only by your choice of media in consuming publications relevant to your profession.

The Source, *Vibe*, XXL, and *The Hype* are Hip-Hop's top magazines. Their pages cover the full spectrum of the Hip-Hop experience: music, fashion, personalities, industry events, politics, business, and beefs. Just like mainstream industry press, these publications host articles from experts, interviews with celebrities, glossy imagery, informative *and* inane reader feedback, and the inescapable advertising that makes it all possible. The light subject matter of *The Source* will make more entertaining, but no less informative, reading than the *New England Journal of Medicine*—assuming that you're studying Hip-Hop, of course . . .

Trade associations were usually founded and funded by companies within a particular slice of the commercial universe. Trade groups advocate for, connect within, and educate on their industry. They tend to be more collegial than competitive, an atmosphere which supports the varied activities of potential and actual competitors in a shared space. The National Association of Manufacturers, the American Medical Association, American Banking Association, the American Farm Bureau, and even the Cremation Association of America all offer some networking and advocacy for professionals doing the job no matter how well-known or obscure it may be.

Think I'm kidding? Even Hip-Hop has its own association: the unimaginatively named Hip-Hop Association. It looks only a little cooler in its abbreviated form: H2A. According to its website, its mission is "to facilitate critical thinking, foster constructive social change and unity to instill tolerance, civic participation, social reform, and economic sustainability, while advancing Hip-Hop's culture through innovative programming."[6] The H2A is not as central to Hip-Hop events and activities as AARP is to senior citizens, but it has its place.

Mentors and social networks within an industry can give managers and entrepreneurs a window into the way things work. If you like your research with a personal touch, get some friends to help you out. It seems like someone always knows someone who gets what you need, the proverbial father's brother's nephew's cousin's former roommate. Leveraging personal networks to make connections with people who know what you need to learn can be as simple as ducking your head in an office down the way or as formal as a carefully brokered introduction with a hired consultant. The Internet can offer you ages of wisdom if used correctly. Social media connections are just a friend request away from knowledgeable business insiders and subject-matter experts. Which links you choose to use depends entirely on how much effort you want to apply to researching your business challenges.

Like a number of artists, Dwayne Michael "Lil Wayne" Carter Jr. decided that there was money in running a record label, so he started up Young Money Entertainment. And one of his crowning achievements with the label was his work mentoring one of Rap's most colorful reigning queens, Nicki Minaj. Onika Tanya "Nicki Minaj" Maraj was born in the Caribbean nation of Trinidad and Tobago and grew up in Queens, New York. Always interested in entertainment, the Islander had a taste for acting and music from a young age. Never totally self-contained, Nicki let her wild side show in her performances. After she released a few singles and mixtapes in 2007 and 2008, Lil Wayne saw Nicki's raw, flamboyant, and sexually suggestive talent as something that could be honed to a fine edge for even greater success in entertainment.

Lil Wayne signed Nicki to Young Money, where he could work with her directly. As the two artists got to know one another, Wayne did what all good mentors do. He helped Nicki refine her lyrical style, using methods he had perfected in his own career, combining word play, metaphors, and punchlines into her music.[7] Lil Wayne did not want to submerge Nicki's style in his own or create a clone. He wanted only to offer her techniques that had been successful for him while providing her the freedom to adapt them as she saw fit.

Not satisfied to simply provide production assistance for Nicki, Lil Wayne provided another great mentoring resource: leveraging a network. Although Nicki had already worked with other artists on her earlier works, he put her on "5 Star Bitch" with Gucci Mane and Trina. The track went gold and ranked #11 on *Billboard's* Hot Rap Songs chart. Success like that opened new doors for Nicki—and for Lil Wayne.

Lil Wayne's mentorship was important but perhaps not essential. Nicki Minaj had talent and drive, qualities that propelled her to the top of the charts with six American Music Awards, ten BET Awards, seven BET Hip-Hop Awards, four Billboard Music Awards, three MTV Video Music Awards, and a number of other honors. However, the mentorship to improve her baseline skills and connect her with other talented and capable people was helpful.

Regardless of which method or combination of means you choose to employ to learn about your industry, you have Hip-Hop's cases to remind you that business research doesn't have to be lame. Hip-Hop doesn't do lame.

I Have a Dream: Mission, Vision, Goals, and Priorities

Mission, vision, goals, and priorities should be the motivating foundations for all activity at work. They are cascading but interrelated concepts and milestones that serve as guideposts for the company's operations. At a business-wide level, vision and mission statements describe what the organization will be and how it will achieve that. They can summarize the organization's aims such as who its operations are supposed to benefit and with what quality levels team members should care for clients. Depending on the effort someone has put into writing the mission statement, values, or vision, the results can range from inspirational to embarrassing corporate plagiarism. For a leader directing people who would rather be doing something else, it is hard to overstate the value of being able to connect the utility of an employee's job to the bigger picture. Mission, vision, and goals (and the tasks to achieve them) create the road map for a team from beginning to end.

I'd like to tell you that there is a lot of science and social engineering that goes into good vision and mission statements, but most are corporate pablum. One is practically indistinguishable from another. They are some sort of mishmash of the words "value," "stakeholders," "first-class," "customer-focused," "quality," and "world domination." In fact, before you and your team begin the agonizing process of sweating every syllable in search of a perfect mission and vision, I encourage you to visit any of the mission- and vision-statement generators that pop to the top of even a superficial Internet search. They can save hours of work by randomly combining power words to do your assignment for you. A corporate mission and vision are valuable to tie together work functions. Strategies and goals are vital to achieve the generalized mission and vision. They should use plain language and be easy for employees to understand and apply.

Hip-Hop is a good place to observe people who have set and met goals in life. Rap's path from its beginnings in underground clubs in New York, with pioneers like Grandmaster Flash, to its central position in mainstream culture, is paved with the milestones of personal achievements, cultural triumphs, and commercial success. Many of Hip-Hop's greatest artists were from poor families, and their rags-to-riches stories are inspiring and exciting. However, their successes at writing, producing, and performing were not some accident. They were the result of a conscious decision to do something. They were the culmination of focus and ambition that we call "goals."

Not every record made, social barrier broken, or studio hit in the history of Hip-Hop was the result of official goal-setting, but a goal-development process can make achieving your dreams more likely.

Annette Richmond is the cofounder and editor of the online newsletter Career-Intelligence.com, providing professional guidance and career advice to thousands of people online. One of her best posts is the guidelines for S.M.A.R.T. Goals:[8]

1. **S**pecific
2. **M**easurable
3. **A**chievable
4. **R**ealistic
5. **T**ime framed

Specific: Direct your energy toward clear-cut ends. A specific goal allows you to concentrate efforts on identifiable tasks that feed into its accomplishment. It should be clear to anyone on the team when they have achieved the goal.

In the early 1990s Marshall "Eminem" Mathers (a.k.a. Slim Shady) decided to get out of Detroit. But why?! Wasn't the Motor City of the late '80s and early '90s awesomeballs? Actually, no. It helps to describe his circumstances at the time to give some context to his specific goal. Mathers had dropped out of high school after three unsuccessful attempts to complete ninth grade. He killed time by working a string of low-paying jobs in fast-food restaurants and factories. He lived in a rental home with his girlfriend, where he was robbed so often (five times) that he started to establish an odd rapport with the burglar: he saw a pattern in the guy making himself peanut butter and jelly sandwiches, how he would move their property out of the house, and his preferred location for fencing goods.[9] Eminem's situation was bad, and, as a goal, leaving Detroit made sense.

Mathers' limited schooling and poor career prospects forced him to create a unique path for himself. With his best friend and early musical mentor, Proof, Mathers created his now-famous alter egos Eminem and Slim Shady. Eminem/Slim Shady/Marshall Mathers knew that White kids from Detroit did not exactly have a fast track to the top of the Hip-Hop hierarchy. Vanilla Ice's controversial and cartoonish performance on the scene (sorry, 'Nilla—not trying to hate—just paraphrasing Eminem) seemed to have poisoned the well for White Hip-Hop artists at the time. Detroit could not compete with L.A. or New York when it came to producing high-profile rappers, in part because there had been virtually no music industry presence there since the decline of Motown a generation earlier. If he was going to make it big, Eminem was first going to have to dominate the local Hip-Hop scene.

After creating what we can call good specific goals (dominating the local Hip-Hop scene and leaving Detroit), all of his work was focused on that task. Eminem and his friends worked extensively, even rearranging work schedules, to make time for writing, performing, and battling in underground clubs like The Shelter until there was no one that could beat him on the Detroit scene.[10] By the time he started to take his act on the road to Hip-Hop competitions elsewhere, he had established himself as the undisputed champion of Detroit clubs.

Measurable: Use numbers to make your goals clearer and actionable. Metrics are the degree to which something is done or not done, and they provide data that can be used to figure out how to fix problems.

Rap was not a well-known genre of music in 1979. It was formed from influences of Soul, Disco, Jamaican DJ dances, and musical sampling,[11] and it was not widely played outside strongholds near New York. Relative to other forms of music at the time, it was completely alien, and that made the likely success of early artists questionable in the eyes of record companies who considered marketing it.

Sylvia Robinson, music producer and founder and CEO of Sugar Hill Records, listened to early Rap in underground clubs. She decided that the hip, new sound could sell, and she wanted her company to be the one to break open the market. She put together a group of performers like Wonder Mike, Master Gee, and Big Bank Hank under the name "The Sugar Hill Gang," and she would sell as many of the group's record, *Rapper's Delight*, as she could. But how would she measure success? The Recording Industry Association of America was the trade organization whose function was the certification of record sales.[12] Albums selling 500,000 copies earned "Gold" status. Sales of 1,000,000 earned "Platinum"; each additional million earned it "Double Platinum," "Triple Platinum," etc. The awards separated the good from the great in a clean and clear-cut manner.

If *Rapper's Delight* could clear half a million records, the music industry and media at large would take notice of the new and unknown genre—and Sugar Hill Records. The profits would clear the way for additional growth at the record label and new albums in a commercially successful Rap category. Like high school students painting a novelty thermometer to mark the progress of a fundraiser, Sugar Hill Records knew exactly how their sales stacked up against their goal. The record eventually went multi-Platinum, far surpassing the initial sales target,[13] and its success was widely credited with launching Hip-Hop onto center stage in the US and abroad.

Achievable: Limit goals to the realm of the possible. There is a delicate balancing act here. Setting objectives beyond your reach can render the goal useless and demotivate you and your team. Conversely, attainable goals can boost morale and inspire further progress on other goals. Consider the resources available like money, social networks, and personal motivation when determining what is achievable.

Initially, Marshall Mathers wanted to become a basketball star in the NBA. Throughout 1990, he played hardcore pickup games at two courts in Detroit. By his own account, Eminem realized that getting into the NBA was "a long shot." In the whole league, there were only about 450 players active on the rosters of the 30 or so teams in the league. In order to achieve his goal, he would be competing against literally tens of thousands of men who were bigger, stronger, faster, more talented, and with greater visibility to team scouts. If things weren't bad enough, Eminem couldn't even beat one of the other regular players who competed in the same pickup games. It did not look good for Marshall Mathers as an NBA star. As a result, he decided that he would refocus his time and energy in an area he thought might be his golden ticket to success: Rap music.[14]

Although being commercially successful in Rap was almost as unlikely as his aspirations for a career in basketball, there were factors that worked in his favor and made his new goal more achievable. Rap was not as physically demanding for a 5'8", 155-pound kid[15] competing against the average NBA player at 6'6" and 221 pounds.[16] Mathers also knew Proof, who was the greatest local talent in Hip-Hop in Detroit. Proof took a special interest in making Eminem into a champion in the battles. Unlike his physical limitations in the realm of professional basketball, artistic and creative efforts were a question of training and time. They were something he could control with the resources available to him.

Realistic: Similar to being achievable, goals need to be reasonable. The goals should be grounded in controllable factors like personal- or bank-financing limits, labor hours available, or thresholds proscribed by law. One method of keeping goals realistic is to base future improvements on past performance, since past performance is a known quantity.

Dana Elaine "Queen Latifah" Owens got a particularly unpleasant phone call. She couldn't believe she was broke. What had happened? Ever since she had made it big in the industry, the money had always been there for her. Music and entertainment had always provided. Latifah made it her goal that she would never let financial disaster sneak up on her again.[17]

She cruised bookstores looking for information on financial management. Latifah decided she would educate herself on how money worked and how it was saved, spent, made, and lost. She researched investment options and then reasserted control over the finances of her company. She recognized it was her money and that she had to be responsible for it.[18]

Latifah set a goal that was completely within her power to achieve: avoiding future financial disaster. By stepping up, she learned from her mistakes in management, cut expenses at the company, and respected the dangers of delegating financial authority without first understanding the nuts and bolts of the business. To date, Latifah's company continues to operate with more black ink than red.

Time framed: Creating goals with time associated with them provides perspective and relevance. Reasonable deadlines can create healthy pressure to continue work and reach goals. Target dates set too far in the future can sap the will to work, and dates set too soon can be unrealistic and depressing when the team can't meet them.

Once, one of Curtis "50 Cent" Jackson's uncles raided his stash and stole roughly $10,000 of raw cocaine. 50 knew that he had to make up the difference fast.[19] When 50 bought drugs from his suppliers, it was on consignment: he didn't own the drugs free and clear. He had to sell what he had in order to cover the cost of the raw materials and hopefully make a profit from a markup when he sold smaller, retail quantities of crack.[20] However, when his uncle pulled that stunt, 50 did not have enough cash to cover the loss to the supplier. He would have to forgo all profit and sell substantially more drugs than usual in order to make up the cost.

Drug dealers who didn't pay suppliers on time didn't have to worry about the minor inconveniences of mainstream market practices like being put on credit hold, calls from collection agencies, or having liens against the business. Delinquent dealers could be found floating face down in the East River or neatly tagged on a slab at the New York City morgue. You'd better believe when 50 Cent set his goal of paying back his supplier, time frame was front and center, and the deadline was coming quick.

50 Cent hustled 24 hours a day for two straight weeks, catching naps on park benches and passing on personal hygiene in order to keep up sales. He couldn't afford to take time off for two main reasons:

1. Junkies wanted to buy crack at all hours of the day and night, whenever the urge hit them. Being absent from the street for any length of time meant sacrificing sales to other dealers when a crackhead needed a fix.
2. The clock was ticking on his repayment, and failure was not an option.

His 336 straight hours of hard work accomplished his goal and bought him a new lease on life since he was able to pay his debt, but 50's uncle would regret putting a target on his nephew's back. 50 laid a beating on him that left no doubt that crossing him was a dangerous and potentially deadly game.

There are never enough hours in the day to do all the things that we want to do—and should. How is someone supposed to repair broken office equipment, do homework, organize a database, check their Facebook profile, call customers, *and* make a cameo appearance in a Drake video all in one day? If the mission, vision, and goals give people a sense of what is important, creating priorities is the best method to differentiate between the weight or value of the things the organization asks them to do.

Setting priorities is racking and stacking the things that make up the goals so that you and your people understand what the most valuable work is. When priorities get out of whack, bad things can happen like poor quality and service, lost customers, injuries, and, ultimately, bankruptcy. Distinguishing between levels of importance is easier said than done because everything is important, but here is something to help with the ranking. The psychologist Abraham Maslow created the pyramid hierarchy of needs which addressed, in order, the requirements and wants of human life. They were from the base to the top physiological, safety, love and belonging, esteem, and self-actualization.

According to the theory, people needed to meet base-level requirements like food, water, and shelter before being able to move on to higher functions of life like love and how good you look in the shower. So how does that relate to work?

In the first place, business has to do two things at a minimum: keep employees and customers safe and legally make money. If a company is injuring people and it is not in the mercenary professions or defense industry, it isn't doing a good job. If a business isn't making money, it won't stay in business long—unless it can get a government bailout. Above these are different degrees of a company's innovation, quality, and service; and above them are issues of reputation, industry prestige, total market share, and corporate citizenship. You can flex some of the higher-level topics to accomplish them simultaneously with things on lower levels, and managers should always feel empowered to adjust priorities if the need arises. Still, it is generally a good idea to ensure that your foundation of business priorities is solid first.

If court records about wage theft, assault, and battery on employees and others are to be believed, Death Row Records might have occasionally violated the first rule of "Do no harm," but let's set that aside for a second. Marion "Suge" Knight wanted to create a powerful, Black-owned entertainment company specializing in Hip-Hop—a clear vision for the organization. He got into the music business to make money, which was in keeping with one of the two base priorities. The label achieved that with three hugely successful albums from Dr. Dre and Snoop Dogg between 1992 and 1994. Death Row looked to expand its product offering by signing and developing more talent. Unfortunately for those artists like Nate Dogg, Lil Bow Wow, and RBX, they didn't have the star power or commercial success that Dre and Snoop did. As a result, Suge weighed his priorities, and making money with a few stars was more important than developing other rappers on the label.

Suge saw that Tupac Shakur, Interscope's star rapper, was doing time in prison without much love from his own label. With two gold and one platinum album, Tupac's popularity promised to make a lot more money than virtually any other artists at Death Row Records. Suge wooed Tupac to leave Interscope, in exchange for legal support to get him out of stir. Once Tupac was in-house, the other artists took second place.

> *Suge told a reporter, "You gotta understand . . . Tupac IS Death Row." Suge's first order of business was to get Afeni [Tupac's mother] a house . . . Suge pampered Tupac and indulged his every whim.*[21]

If album sales were the measure of successful prioritization, then Tupac's first album with Death Row, *All Eyez on Me,* was a grand slam with a diamond certification at more than 10,000,000 sold. The priority shuffle might not have been good for second-tier artists, but it was good for Death Row.

Priorities, goals, missions, and vision statements give leaders and their people clarity on what needs to happen, and they help an organization plot a course over long periods of time. S.M.A.R.T. goals are just one method to use goals to direct a team, and managers should feel free to mix and match goal-setting methods. Priorities should be rough guidelines and not inflexible suicide pacts that can never be changed. Whether the company meets its objectives or not, just having the markers described here allows leaders to measure success or failure, and that counts for something.

The Source Begins: Business Plans

You've done research into the kind of business you'd like to be in, and you've got your vision, mission, goals, and priorities set. You're going to need to make a business plan. The idea is that your proposal will map out your strategy for world domination and get you the financing that the business will need. The basics of a business plan include a market strategy, a management concept, and a financial plan.

The market strategy should provide a map of the who's, what's, and where's of your business, products, and services in the marketplace. It identifies actual or potential competitors, customers, and how you plan to raise awareness of your product, fend off rivals, and attract clients.

Your management concept includes the nuts and bolts of day-to-day operations. It contains details on the structure and responsibilities of company employees, supervision, and management. The section should address business logistics and supplier administration.

The financial plan is how you are going to pay for all of it. This critical piece of the business plan is home to product costing, payroll, and capital requirements that your banker and investors will want to review as a sanity check. While shortcomings in any part of a business plan can sink a business even before launch, weaknesses in the financial plan can be the biggest indicator of trouble ahead.

The Source was to Hip-Hop media what *The New York Times* was to print news. It was the granddaddy to later Hip-Hop journalistic arrivals on the scene like *Vibe, XXL,* and the myriad of online Hip-Hop news and gossip sites. Founded by Dave Mays and Jon Shecter as a one-page spread to promote their radio show at Harvard, the two grew the business to be the preeminent Hip-Hop media outlet.

In 1988, there wasn't a lot of competition for readers in the Hip-Hop realm. In fact, the other magazines targeting the youth demographic didn't have any focus on Hip-Hop as a niche at all. Shecter and Mays' marketing plan did not need to place much emphasis on beating the competition since there was none. The way the two roommates plotted the customer base for Rap fans was by creating a database of the names and addresses of callers to their radio program. They were able to use the database as a sales tool to prove to advertisers that there were plenty of potential customers to be reached. They knew that as their fan base and revenue grew, *The Source* could reach more customers nationwide, so the marketing strategy reflected that.

The management concept began simply enough. For an office, Mays and Shecter worked out of their dorm. They arranged printing and mailings of *The Source* with local printshops. They created plans to divide the work. They split marketing, budgeting, production, distribution, events, and writing between them. Over time, they planned to bring on reporters to cover events and conduct interviews with insiders, DJs, and artists. The founders knew that they would need to move to more suitable offices as operations picked up, and the management concept had that contingency covered.[22]

Mays and Shecter's financial plan was conservative since they had their doubts about the likelihood of success in launching a Hip-Hop magazine. Since no major media companies were gunning for the Hip-Hop audiences, banks were reluctant to provide financing to *The Source*. They were just unwilling to gamble on Rap. As a result, the founders planned to fund themselves, so they budgeted to collect advertising and subscription fees as quickly as possible . . . even before distributing the magazine.[23] Only once *The Source* had established itself and could show positive sales results did the banks come around to see Hip-Hop print media as a legitimate business worthy of their funding.

A good business idea, solid research, and a well-written plan can put you on track to overcome significant odds and reach the commercial big leagues. Think about it: most people wouldn't have picked a couple of White kids from Harvard as the founding fathers of Hip-Hop media, but planning goes a long way toward beating the odds.

The Rap Name Generator: Branding the Business

Hip-Hop knows how to name things: Andre 3000, Salt-N-Pepa, Ghostface Killah, Shorty Sh1tstain . . . Well, maybe Hip-Hop isn't *perfect* when it comes to names, but who is? Let's take a look at the considerations that go into the process. A name imbues a business with personality and character in a flash, so choosing something that fits what you want your organization to be is important without stepping on someone else's toes with trademark infringement.

The name will affect how your potential customers see you, so start the naming process with the customer in mind. Think of N.W.A. (Niggaz Wit Attitudes), the most famous pioneers of Gangsta Rap. To call their band name edgy is a bit of an understatement, but its aggressiveness was exactly the impression that Dr. Dre, DJ Yella, MC Ren, Arabian Prince, and Ice Cube wanted to give listeners in the mid- to late 1980s as their new style of Rap raged onto the scene. The name's in-your-face countercultural statement attracted a youthful, assertive, and nonconformist demographic in a way that the name "Vanilla Ice" never would. The group followed up with over-the-top, hardcore lyrics in their music.

Ahmir "Questlove" Thompson and Tariq "Black Thought" Trotter of The Roots attracted a different group of Hip-Hop fans with the serene names they chose for themselves and their band. Even before new listeners heard their eclectic sound, the names set an expectation that The Roots would likely have a less-militant sound compared to N.W.A., and that fact was either a good thing or a bad thing depending on what kind of fan the band was trying to attract.

Because of the trends in globalization and market liberalization, the commercial world is a crowded place. Although the English language seems to expand by the hour with new words and slang, sometimes it is hard to come up with a name that doesn't infringe on someone else's trademark or brand name. A trademark is a recognizable design, sign, or expression protected by law which distinguishes one company's product or service from others'.

William Leonard Roberts II, more commonly recognized as the hulking, bearded, Florida-raised rapper Rick Ross, has had his share of name trouble. After being in the Hip-Hop spotlight for years, artist Rick Ross was sued for $10 million by "Freeway" Rick Ross, a notorious Los Angeles-based drug kingpin who had served a 13-year sentence after being convicted.[24] Freeway claimed that Roberts had stolen the high-rolling, larger-than-life name and gangster persona that he had created in the course of his years-long career selling more than $900 million in narcotics. The lawsuit threatened to disrupt the artist's release of his album *Teflon Don*, which would have been a huge financial setback to Roberts, since he needed the album out on the street to generate sales.

Fortunately for the artist, Rick Ross, the suit was dismissed in a matter of weeks with the legal support of his record label making it possible for *Teflon Don* to ultimately be a certified gold record.[25] The lesson is that a simple Internet word search and some discretion in picking your name can save a lot of trouble down the road.

Hip-Hop and the Digital Encounter: Online Presence

As the music industry consolidated in search of lower costs and higher profits, breakout success via the traditional route for new artists went from difficult to near-NBA-draft-lottery-winner remote. It was hard to get picked up when there were fewer and fewer avenues to the big time. But luckily for Hip-Hop artists, social media was taking off at the same time as the belt-tightening of record companies. Emcees, DJs, and entertainers of all stripes found free online outlets to promote themselves and their music directly to fans.

Lil Wayne, Gucci Mane, and Kanye West all took to the sea of shifting tastes in social media to attract followers without the intermediaries at the record labels. They could communicate with their devotees, giving them the feeling of proximity and authenticity that was tough to achieve in the early days of the genre. Yes, online and social media presence changed the game for Hip-Hop.

At its core, the Internet serves to connect, inform, and attract people. But for businesses, virtual spaces allow them to promote their brands in a way that transcends the traditional limitations of physical location, geography, and telephonic and mailing communications. The software offers businesses data and analytics on clients and their behavior automatically in a way never before achieved. An online presence is an equalizing gateway to global commerce. The online outlets available for companies to reach people are beyond easy description or categorization. But the immensity of platform options and the infinite ways to engage customers need not be overwhelming. Just answering the questions "Where are your clients?" "What do they need?" and "What kind of experience can I offer?" practically writes the plan for your online and social media presence.

Know where your customers are, and meet them there. This assumes that you know who your customers are as part of the market research of a business plan. It is always a safe bet to create a website for the business. As one of the oldest Internet manifestations, a website can serve as an online backstop, which advertises your existence, personality, and mission. A well-designed, functional, and simple website can serve as a direct link between your business and the customer. A user should be only a click or two away from your contact information. Big business, spam traps, and porn sites have long since claimed all the best web addresses like molestationnursery.com, gotahoenorth.com, or therapistinabox.com; but a company can still stand out online by using appropriate metatags to make it easy for search engines to find them and pass along to clients.

Your customers are on social media, but the real question is "Where?" Tumblr, Facebook, LinkedIn, Whatsapp, Twitter, Instagram, or China's Facebook equivalent, Renren, all attract a particular kind of user. The mainline social media companies have worked hard to market their products, and a quick search can net articles describing the popularity of each one with different demographics. The description or image you developed of your likely customers and their social media of choice should give you an idea where to stake your claim to draw them in.

Each social media site contains some instructions for getting started, sometimes with additional services to help businesses optimize their presence. The downside is that a fair number of these companies recognize that if you are connecting with them for advice, you're probably willing to pay for it. A cheaper route is to use the vast quantities of free online advice in the form of videos and blogs on optimizing any social media platform. Even veteran users of social media can benefit from the occasional review of the trends mentioned in the optimization "how-to" posts.

Present what the client needs. People part with their money only if they believe that you can help them with something. Keeping that problem-solving concept at the forefront of site design is critical to a successful online presence. Again, your market research should tell you what your clients want, whether it is information, goods, or kinky sexual services. Your task is to package it for easy consumption by the customer.

The fundamentals of online presence are well-designed, functional, and simple. The "well-designed" part sometimes depends on how talented or creative you or your team are or how big your budget is for outside support. Spending a bit more here can often have an outsized effect on customers. It might cost hundreds of thousands or millions of dollars to renovate or upgrade physical offices, stores, plants, or facilities. However, having a visually impressive social media setup or website may cost only a few hundred or thousand dollars. That cost differential is significant. Since your online presence might be the only thing many clients may see, make it count.

Functional and simple are two sides to the same coin. Good looks don't mean much if the service isn't good. Excessive advertisements, broken web links, incomplete/incorrect information, and/or difficult-to-navigate fields can send customers running for the online exits like dealers from a drug bust. No matter what you decide to put on your social media and websites, test it with several people and make sure that it works on various devices and via different navigational approaches. The feedback you get will make your service more attractive to real customers.

Consider the customer experience. Similar to how your market research should tell you who your likely customers are and what they want, you need to know how to give it to them. Your online and social media presence allows you to remain in near constant contact with customers—sometimes whether you like it or not. Adding a comments section or contact info keeps the lines of communication open. Use the feedback you get from your users to fix your problems and address their concerns.

It wasn't long after the social media revolution started that the avenues to stardom that propelled the likes of 50 Cent to the top tier of entertainment success were choked with other social media wannabees. The inexpensive, non-traditional route to fame and fortune was clogged with every rapper with a digital camera and a YouTube login. Getting recognition was hard again, maybe even harder than before.

Seeing that aspiring artists lacked a way to stand out amid the massive and noisy traffic online, a few Hip-Hop fans decided there was a hole in the digital market. They founded Stopthebreaks. com, an independent marketing and promotion platform dedicated to advancing Hip-Hop entertainers. They used their tech savvy in multiple media platforms like Pinterest, Facebook, Twitter, StumbleUpon, and Google+ to help artists to be heard over the din of competing voices.

Their online presence was relatively consistent from platform to platform. Their base website was attractive and understated with trademark black and white. The links leading from section to section flowed smoothly, with most information only a click or two away from any part, making navigation easy for users. They folded in audio and video seamlessly with their text. They engaged their followers in comments and posts with a balance of light humor and effective communication.

Stopthebreaks' wizardry can't guarantee every new artist a record contract and piles of cash. But their effective application of online marketing principles and proficiency with nearly all of the mainline social media platforms help give new DJs, emcees, producers and managers a fighting chance to get noticed.

THE HUSTLERS' GAME:
SALES AND MARKETING

SALES AND MARKETING have always been part of Hip-Hop culture. When Hip-Hop was just starting to take off, rappers used to make reference to their favorite products in their songs. Run-DMC's 1986 smash single "My Adidas" was art reflecting life, and the band's plug for the three-striped kicks did plenty for the athletic shoe manufacturer's revenue at a time when it needed a boost. It was a real treat since Adidas hadn't even asked for the endorsement.

Over time, Hip-Hop artists and entrepreneurs decided to plug their own brands and products rather than those of third-party companies. Russell Simmons created the Phat Farm clothing line. Jay-Z and Damon Dash created Armadale Vodka. Oh, and Wiz Khalifa created his own Khalifa Kush marijuana strain, but given some of its legal hang-ups, the product's sales are hard to track . . .

Businesses exist to solve people's problems and make money. Marketing and sales are the methods used to make people aware of your business, products, and services. They are the means by which you get money out of your customers' pockets and into yours. As always, we'll let Hip-Hop teach us some of the basics in our quest to understand the sources of revenue.

You Down with OPPPP? Product, Place, Price, and Promotion

People buy what they value, and marketing is the means to communicate the value of a product. Marketing happens to be Hip-Hop's strongest attribute. From its birth as a minor music-scene subculture with a few hundred followers to its present-day globe-straddling reach, Hip-Hop marketing created value for its fans (perhaps better described in this case as customers): the need to be cool. Hip-Hop artists and entrepreneurs created everything about Hip-Hop to meet the need for *cool,* a term vague and broad enough to fit into lots of different definitions. At almost any point in its history, the genre itself was a break from more mainstream music, which bestowed the "cool" status by virtue of being different. The raw messages in political Rap were true for some listeners, which qualified as "cool" for them. Then there were the clothes, cars, cash, and cribs of the artists, and those material demonstrations of success and style had their own kind of "cool." The list goes on. Hip-Hop's ability to create value for its consumers is a textbook example of good marketing.

In order for marketing to be successful, it has to hit on all of the elements of good marketing, which are sometimes called the four Ps: Product, Place, Price, and Promotion.

Product speaks to the actual goods or services for sale, and they answer some customer demand. They are the things you might commonly buy like clothes, haircuts, cell phones, tattoos, and/or germanium tetrachloride (you know, for when you're making fiber-optic cladding at home . . .). You get them because you want them or you need them, no matter for how brief a time. If you didn't, you wouldn't have spent your money, and things wouldn't be filling closets, drawers, and a growing number of hard-to-explain storage centers. Just like the Hip-Hop example of selling cool, businesses need to find the market demand that makes its goods and services valuable to the consumer.

Anyone who has ever come across ancient photos of early Hip-Hop fashion gets an immediate appreciation of the product life cycle. Goods and style-driven services are born, grow old, and eventually die a merciful death like Hammer pants, most DMX music, or tiny cell phones. What starts out as a hot new thing on the scene, setting record sales, can quickly age into eye-rolling irrelevance to the market, leaving costly, unsold inventory. As a result, companies have to consider the arc of a product's life as part of marketing in order to define its service broadly enough to adapt to technological advances or changes in consumer styles and tastes. A stylist or barber will learn to create new hairstyles rather than go out of business when high-top fades and beehives fall out of fashion. Similarly, even as businesses create new products, they need to prepare for the eventual maturity and decline of them with still newer products and services.

The second P of marketing is place. Despite the name, place need not actually relate to a particular location. Instead, it centers on the logistics of sales.

1. Where does the business make its products: domestically, in-house, overseas, or third-party manufacturing?
2. What are the channels of distribution and sales: company-owned stores, franchises, agents, call centers, or online?

If marketing is about creating value for customers, then place needs to benefit them through convenience and cost.

In Hip-Hop's early days, most clubs developing and playing Rap were small, local venues in New York boroughs. They were inaccessible to large numbers of potential fans. However, mixtapes took the music from the club to the streets and neighborhoods, giving the pioneer artists wider circulation. Eventually radio boosted Hip-Hop's exposure to the wider world, taking it into the lucrative suburban market, where sales exploded. More recently, file sharing and social media expanded even further the reach of Hip-Hop to any point on Earth with Internet access and even space, with satellite uplink. The evolution of distribution from music available only in clubs on weekends to mixtapes sold hand-to-hand, through to streaming music available on any device at any time shows how Hip-Hop met the customer demand for convenience and low cost in marketing's place.

Price is the most easily recognized element of marketing. It is frequently the first thing a customer thinks of when considering a product. How much a business charges clients for goods and services affects the likelihood of sales and the overall profitability of the operation. Price changes with a number of variables, including available supply and the perceived value.

The Club Paradise Tour of 2012 grossed $42 million over the course of 60 shows in North America and Europe, and fans consider it one of the best concert tours in Hip-Hop history. Drake, Nicki Minaj, Meek Mill, A$AP Rocky, Kendrick Lamar, 2 Chainz, and Wocka Flocka Flame all worked their magic on the stage at venues regularly accommodating upwards of 10,000 fans. Here we have an excellent opportunity to see marketing pricing in action.

In late February 2012, the Frank C. Erwin Jr. Special Events Center in Austin, Texas, hosted Club Paradise with nearly 12,000 tickets for sale. Given the popularity of the combined performers, Hip-Hop fans saw the concert as a must-see event, and marketers took advantage of the occasion. The limited seating in the VIP areas sold to high rollers for $1,700 a seat. Even the cheap seats weren't cheap at north of $125 each, and those sold out quickly. Despite the sky-high prices and totally lame Monday-night scheduling, 97% of the venue sold out. The lesson here is that when customers perceive scarcity and value, they are willing to pay a premium to be part of it.

Marketing's promotion is a customer-focused process used to recognize and attract customers to build and sustain the business. It can be about increasing a product's or brand's profile or improving customer loyalty. Promotion includes sales organization, advertising, and public relations.

How a business structures sales can have a huge impact on revenues. Some companies rely on distributors and product representatives to handle actual sales, preferring to leave *finding* customers to a third party. Other organizations conduct their business over the Internet, providing some distance between the company and the customer in the interest of reducing costs. The most familiar method of sales organization involves actual person-to-person connections. These are the salespeople talking directly to customers in stores, on the phone, or out in the field covering regional territories. The arrangement of the sales force depends on the product and a balance between the most convenient and cost-effective way to reach the customer.

In Hip-Hop, artists had to be flexible in how they handled sales of their music. Most of the grandfathers of Rap started their musical careers as independent salesmen. They sold mixtapes out of their cars, performed at friends' parties, and did gigs at small clubs. Their reach went only as far as the people in front of them. Once the artist got a little recognition and a decent manager, the manager could serve in a sales-administration capacity, organizing events and promotion. The sales force expanded and, so, too, did the artist's reach. If and when the artist made the big time with a record deal at a good label, the label's sales and distribution force took over the events, promotion, and sales, using their larger and more-specialized resources to help push album sales nationwide and sometimes worldwide. The artists and managers still had to do their part writing, recording, producing, and performing, but with the means available to record labels and entertainment companies, the job of reaching wider and wider audiences was easier than at the beginning.

Although they have some things in common, advertising and public relations are not the same thing. Advertising makes information and materials to support sales. You see these in pop-up ads on the web, billboards, commercials, and even the unfortunate human advertisements spinning signs in front of Cash-for-Gold exchanges. Public relations create messages supporting the organization, and others spread them through the infinitely variable means of communication available to people: word of mouth, electronically via social media and traditional media outlets, and even through government propaganda.

Favoring either advertising or public relations has its advantages and disadvantages. Having both is the best of both worlds. OutKast's *Speakerboxxx/The Love Below*, managed to achieve that. Andre Lauren "Andre 3000" Benjamin and Antwan Andre "Big Boi" Patton rejoined forces in 2003 to create an experimental fifth album after working as solo artists. When the leadership at OutKast's label, Arista, heard the tracks, they recognized the potential for crossover hits. Arista spent significantly to give the double album the best possible chance for commercial success, financing five videos and launching two singles, "Hey Ya" and "The Way You Move." In addition to these, Arista spent on the usual advertising material that accompanied album releases at the time, like in-store CD display endcaps for high visibility.

The real success for *Speakerboxxx/The Love Below* came through public relations. Andre 3000 and Big Boi hit the media circuit, conducting interviews with anyone who would talk to them, getting their story out to the fans/consumers. The video and singles releases blew up almost overnight with radio- and Internet-traffic-setting records. The album sold 510,000 copies in the first week, and the album's success took on a life of its own—PR at its finest. Fans talked and posted to one another feverishly. Critics raved about the band, the musical style, the lyrics—anything and everything. Arista and Outkast didn't have to do anything else. The PR was a positive self-fulfilling prophecy which went a long way toward making *Speakerboxxx/The Love Below* the most successful Hip-Hop album ever with more than 11 million units sold and certified diamond by the Recording Industry Association of America.

Hip-Hop "Strategery": Marketing Tactics

If marketing strategies are the road maps to achieve commercial goals, Hip-Hop had that covered from jump. The innovators of the musical genre somehow just knew what had to be done at every turn of the changing times to capture the attention of their audience, grow the market, and make a lot of green. Their strategies, like any good business, could and did change depending on market conditions. Whether artists were first-in, me-too, or niche players, they all had their own way of seizing the spotlight. Each style has its strengths and weaknesses, and looking at those methods is a good way to spend a few pages.

Pioneers who plant the flag in a new market get the status of first-in. They can control resources and shape the terrain in a way that late arrivals cannot. First-in competitors enjoy at least a brief monopoly of the market, and they can demand premiums because of that. The challenge for those first-in businesses is similar to old-timey pioneers: there is a lot of work to be done to control the landscape. First-in companies have to promote their advantage with customers who may be unaware of the new product or services or what advantages they may have. They have to fight through the inevitable hiccups associated with new launches. First-mover advantages last only so long. If the market is attractive enough, it is only a matter of time before the me-too players start showing up.

In the late 1970s, Black music was in a bit of a rut compared to the golden age of Motown, brighter times for R&B, or even the popularity bump of early Disco. Onto that musical wasteland Rap appeared as an experimental new sound. It was initially just a subculture on the club scene in New York City, but the Sugar Hill Gang and their hit single "Rapper's Delight" changed all of that with marketing tactics that were typical of first-in enterprises. The rhythmic, spoken-word song performed to a danceable beat was unlike anything on the scene at the time. The band's trio, Michael "Wonder Mike" Wright, Henry "Big Bank Hank" Jackson, and Guy "Master Gee" O'Brien, brought energy and innovation to a market that was hungry for something new to satisfy its need for novelty after other sounds had gone stale. When Sugar Hill Records pressed up and sold the records, they took off. Audiences far afield of the New York clubs and discos were hearing Hip-Hop for the first time, and they were eating it up. The song broke into the Top 40. Sales of the single topped $2 million, with the label collecting $3.5 million in revenue— not too shabby for a genre that few people knew existed just a couple years earlier.

Giving the Sugar Hill Gang their due, "Rapper's Delight" had its charm. Rap was a new sound for the world. The beat was easy to follow for untrained ears, and the lyrics were catchy. It made it easy for young people unfamiliar with it to cross over and experience the strange, new music. If we define the terms broadly enough, we can say that Sugar Hill brought a kind of technological leadership with their new sound.

"Rapper's Delight" demanded attention from listeners who were tired of their clichéd musical alternatives, making the audience drift to Hip-Hop, possibly demonstrating the principle of asset preemption; and for that, generations of Rap fans owe Wonder Mike, Big Bank Hank, and Master Gee a debt of gratitude.

However, like other marketing pioneers, Sugar Hill Gang had their limitations. Unlike most other genres of music, there wasn't much vocal talent required to Rap. There were no hard-to-hit high notes, no harmonies to coordinate, no complex instrumental accompaniment. Anyone listening to "Rapper's Delight" could learn the words quickly, and anyone with rhythm and the ability to rhyme could get in the game. In short, there were virtually no barriers to enter into the Rap game, and the popularity of the sound and the commercial success of the single made it a model to be replicated by others. Sugar Hill Gang never managed to follow up "Rapper's Delight" with any comparable hits. And as the field of competing artists expanded quickly, they passed into artistic obscurity.

Me-too competitors have the advantage of seeing what did and did not work for the pioneers in the first place, but in order to be successful, there are obligations that come with late entrants. They have to make improvements based on customer feedback and their own research and development in order to offer something new, novel, or better than what came before. The me-too position must find ways to cut costs and offer the customer savings since they generally do not have the same power to set prices to the same degree that pioneers did.

No Hip-Hop artist (and no record label, for that matter) wants to compete on price. It would fly in the face of the material aspirations of Hip-Hop for the "good life"; and, for the publicly traded entertainment companies already under financial pressure, additional losses of margin brought on by lower selling prices are unacceptable. However, that still leaves the innovation and service routes wide open to the me-too competitors in Hip-Hop, and that has been the continuing story of the musical genre.

Stanley "MC Hammer" Burrell built his flashy attire and dance routines to accompany his hits like "U Can't Touch This" and "2 Legit 2 Quit" in the late 1980s. His now famous Hammer pants and onesie jumpsuits were trademark items for him, which partially made the MC Hammer brand. Although Hammer had some unique elements that differentiated him from his contemporaries, he was a classic me-too in the market.

His music was a variation on the already successful commercialized music and acts inside and outside of Hip-Hop. Run DMC and LL Cool J both offered templates for his path into commercial music and entertainment. He certainly wasn't the first to do so, but Hammer sampled heavily from other artists like Prince, Rick James, and The Jackson 5 to create his own hits. Despite some similarities to other acts, Hammer brought enough value to the studio and the stage to make his popularity soar over his first few albums. By late in his career, he had sold 50 million records. Hammer experienced a career arc from poverty on the streets of Oakland to the entourage-fueled, gold-plated excesses that frequently precede a precipitous decline back down the economic ladder. Eventually, his overexposure and inability to innovate beyond pop-friendly jingles caused Hammer to lose market share to acts like Eazy-E's N.W.A. and Ice-T, which provided a whole new sound and image for Hip-Hop: Gangsta Rap.

Gangsta Rap had its time in the sun generating Hip-Hop icons like 2Pac Shakur, Biggie Smalls, and Snoop Dogg; but despite their differences from the acts that came before them, they were me-too competitors as well. No matter how good Gangsta Rap was, it, too, gave way little by little to newer images and sounds like the bling and self-laudatory sounds of P Diddy or the saccharine dance hits of the Dirty South. It just goes to show that, with a little creativity to provide some market differentiation, even me-too competitors can clear new spaces in a crowded market.

From a marketing-strategy perspective, the me-too competitors don't have the same risk as first-in pioneers. The obligations for innovation or research and development can be somewhat easier having had others to blaze a trail, make mistakes, and generally show the world how it's done. Sometimes the marketplace is so crowded that competing across the full spectrum of product offerings is impossible or at least very difficult. A new vehicle manufacturer would find it difficult to offer every option from a moped to a city bus on their first day in business. Limiting the focus of a business to a particular niche can enable it to provide value through specialization. Harley Davidson is an iconic brand who succeeded selling in a niche. Rather than trying to offer a wide selection of dirt bikes, sport bikes, or crotch rockets, Harley Davidson billed itself as manufacturer of large-displacement motorcycles designed specifically for street driving. And they were rewarded for their success focusing within the niche by their rabidly loyal customers who were not only willing to buy their bikes from them but to actually brand themselves for life with Harley tattoos.

Hip-Hop has its niche bands, but few stand out better than The Roots. Outsiders even in the early days of Hip-Hop, Ahmir "Questlove" Thompson and Tariq "Black Thought" Trotter started their group in the late 1980s. For one thing, they were from Philadelphia, a city slightly off Hip-Hop's beaten path when compared to the genre's capital cities at the time in Los Angeles and New York. Unlike many Hip-Hop artists, Questlove and Black Thought had a leg up in education, attending the highly respected magnet school, Philadelphia High School for the Creative and Performing Arts. The lessons they learned there and from Questlove's musician parents gave them a taste for a wide variety of music. In The Roots, they created jazz-influenced sounds. They added live instrumentals, complex rhyme arrangements, and intricate lyricism to their music.

Compared to the other albums in Hip-Hop, The Roots were out of the mainstream, and Questlove explains how that niche sound worked to their advantage.

> We also benefitted, I think, from being positioned as counterprogramming to the dominant forces in Hip-Hop, which were perceived as moving toward the extremes of commercialism . . . We were embraced because of what we weren't. Add to that the fact that there was a void in conscious Hip-Hop . . . and our elevation made sense. Authenticity was in short supply . . . We filled a niche.[1]

Even if they were never the biggest act in Hip-Hop, The Roots have managed to stay relevant to large numbers of fans for decades. And to prove that point, they've been nominated for a hella long list of awards. They won three Grammy Awards and three NAACP Image Awards. They sold millions of albums, earned gold- and platinum-certified records, and Questlove participated in the production of the hit Broadway musical *Hamilton*. It is fair to say that their niche marketing paid off for The Roots.

Marketing strategies can give successful direction to business operations, no matter where a company is in the spectrum of competitors. First-in innovators, me-too followers, and niche architects can all capture the attention of the audience, grow the market, and make a lot of green when they know their roles and adapt to changing circumstances. But not everyone always recognizes when times are changing in the market.

Straight Outta Compton: Changes in Marketing

Nothing stays the same for very long, and realizing that something is happening is the first step to adapting to change. Back in the day, the traditional mold of rappers in the mid- to late '80s included heavy leather cladding and/or nylon tracksuits. These were typical clothes on album covers at the time. The delicate sensibilities of television and radio broadcasters of the time kept performers on a relatively tame lyrical track. After five or six years of similar Rap music and style, the audience wanted something new.

Not every Rap act, their managers, or the record labels recognized the need for a change. While the record sales for safe (if stagnant) acts like T La Rock and Spoonie Gee didn't hurt the bottom line of the labels producing their albums, they weren't exactly making it rain, either. The traditional record labels of the time had been slow to embrace Hip-Hop in the first place. Even with the demonstrated commercial success of their signed Rap artist, labels could not predict what direction Hip-Hop might take.

The commercial rise of West Coast Gangsta Rap should have been no surprise to entertainment-savvy professionals, but it was. The unbelievable success of the contemporary television show *Miami Vice* was due to its portrayal and glorification of sex, music, drugs, money, and violence. The public yearned for it, which justified more than $100 million in production costs that the show incurred over the life of the series.[2] *Miami Vice*'s popularity as a fictionalized account of the drug war should have had a quicker effect in the music business.

One could argue that Gangsta Rap artists like Tracy "Ice-T" Marrow, Eric "Eazy-E" Wright, and Andre "Dr. Dre" Young packaged the same, or at least similar, content as *Miami Vice* in Hip-Hop music and delivered it to the consumer. Where Don Johnson and Philip Michael Thomas connected with affluent, White, suburban youth as actors playing cops in South Florida, Ice-T and other Gangsta Rappers reached the same demographic as edgy, modern anti-heroes from L.A. In that respect, Rap's movement (or continued movement) beyond predominantly Black, urban markets into other cultural or ethnic demographics is understandable. After all, in business you can't go wrong targeting people with money to spend.

Revolutions in the market can occasionally come out of left field, but more often than not, there are early signs of change before the marketplace is upended that perceptive professionals can look for. After a few weeks on the air, *Miami Vice*'s success was no secret. There were articles in newspapers, magazines, and entertainment publications. Nightly news broadcasts did features on the show's scandalous sex and gratuitous violence. The Nielsen ratings, television's gold standard for popular feedback, showed that *Miami Vice* was a hit.

When it comes to Gangsta Rap, record companies could have done a better job tracking the musical bellwethers in Hip-Hop's incubators: the clubs, street corners, and house parties where kids had been testing out new music since the beginning of Rap. While these sources of market intelligence were not as easily accessible to record-label managers as published Neilsen ratings or articles in *The Washington Post*, they were not unknown to music-industry professionals.

As we've said earlier, every industry has its social networks and trade publications that can provide insight into market trends, and smart professionals monitor them at least occasionally for market opportunities and disruptive changes. True mavens will go beyond those traditional means of market intelligence to find whatever their industry equivalents are to the clubs, street corners, and house parties of Hip-Hop. Companies that adapt to changes survive and thrive.

Fundamentals of Slinging: Sales Techniques

Marketing research and strategy set the table for sales to serve up the products and services to customers, and that brings in the cash. But before a company can count its green, there are still steps in the sales process to accomplish, including contacting customers, building rapport, searching for pain, negotiating and closing, and getting referrals.

Until artificial intelligence totally eradicates humanity, people are still going to do most of the purchasing on the planet. That means that business professionals will have to know how to connect to customers as humans first. And there are lots of ways to contact potential customers: person-to-person, hosting training or community events, online and through social media, and, if you're looking to go retro, there is always direct mail.

Say what you will about his music, his style, or his ego, Sean "P Diddy" Combs was a good salesman. He knew how to cover the full spectrum of the sales process. In his early years, he was famous for promoting events and attracting crowds of 1,000 people or more. His trademark parties were at Daddy's House on West 54th Street in Manhattan, hosting heavyweight Hip-Hop artists of the day like A Tribe Called Quest, Big Daddy Kane, and members of Run DMC.

Diddy used several techniques to attract guests. He made calls to tastemakers, emcees, and DJs he knew would get the word out for him. He got spots placed on the radio and posters placed in high-traffic areas. Diddy did some of his best work in person. He used his personal charm and charisma handing out flyers to total strangers on the streets in neighborhoods where Hip-Hop fans lived to drum up enthusiasm for whatever event he was promoting.

While the goal of contact with clients might be to generate revenue, effective customer relationships require a balance between human connection and the satisfying of business needs. That leads to our next two points: building rapport and searching for pain.

Professionals have to understand people. Personal courtesy and knowing what matters to a customer is the basis for building the rapport that enables a good business relationship. Good manners like greeting people politely, saying "Please" and "Thank you," and speaking respectfully are the sorts of things your mother should have taught you, and they work wonders for customer service. After all, who doesn't like nice people? Knowing what matters to clients can be the superficial things that sustain the stereotypes of backslapping, glad-handing salesmen. Lighthearted topics might be someone's favorite team or the weather. With deeper relationships, salespeople can speak to more intimate subjects like family, health, hopes, or dreams. Having good, personal exchanges helps to humanize both the salesperson and the customer, which should help smooth the sales process. Customers are more likely than not to buy from people they like or feel connected to.

It is possible to overdo it when trying to build rapport. There is a danger in oversharing about yourself or prying deeply into a customer's life. Customers barely want salespeople in their lives. They definitely don't want potential stalkers . . .

Jonathan "Lil Jon" Smith had the upbringing and personality that made building rapport easy for him. The Crunk-style Hip-Hop star, famous for his dreadlocks and one-word lyrical plugs, was raised in a well-to-do neighborhood near Atlanta, Georgia. That afforded him access to a wide range of people, cultures, and activities. As a charismatic and personable youth, he developed a multi-ethnic crew of friends. The skaters introduced him to Punk bands. Other friends started him on Reggae and Dancehall music.

Lil Jon did not force himself way outside his comfort zone to do what he did. He took in all kinds of music because he honestly liked trying new things. This gave him something that he could use to connect with new people. Lil Jon had the ability to relate to different people and focus on them and their interests with casual conversations based on his own leisure activities. And that made it easy for him to network and build relationships.[3]

Initially, his friendly connections just got him small gigs DJ-ing at parties at his place or elsewhere. "By inviting over his different cliques and getting them drunk, he won a reputation for throwing banging parties. 'I was the hottest DJ in Atlanta.'"[4]

With time, his deepening contacts translated into his first record deal with Mirror Image Records and the release of *Get Crunk, Who U Wit*. Two singles off the album made it onto the *Billboard* Top 100. Lil Jon used his rapport-building skills, based on his own interests, over time to successfully branch out into solo and acting work.

The only reason that people spend money is to solve problems. Think about it. We buy medicines to cure ailments. We pay for entertainment as the solution to boredom. And we adopt rescue dogs to fix the nagging problems associated with our unchewed shoes and furniture, feces-free floors, and perhaps the odd bit of loneliness. Searching for pain means learning about customers' problems with the intent to create solutions to them through your products and services.

Elements of pain can be minor, like a few extra seconds to check out at a store, an ugly website, or not liking your pre-printed fate in a fortune cookie. A customer's pain can also be much more serious, like poor-quality products, high prices, or God-awful response times (I'm looking at you, home-renovation contractors . . .) A good salesperson will find out the sources of pain and craft methods to reduce or eliminate the customer's frustrations. Are there ways your company can offer the customer a better experience?

The hulking former NFL player Marion "Suge" Knight was famous for his work building the Gangsta Rap icon, Death Row Records. The label attracted some great artists in Hip-Hop under his early leadership: Dr. Dre, Snoop Dogg, Warren G, and Lady of Rage. Although Suge is more famous for inflicting pain than searching for it, Death Row would never have landed Tupac Shakur without Suge's recognition of what the talented, if troubled, young artist needed.

Tupac grew up in a family of 1960s-era revolutionaries. Moving from the East Coast to the West Coast in the 1980s, he was in a position to launch an artistic career with hardcore yet occasionally poetic hits that spoke to Hip-Hop fans. His first three albums, *2Pacalypse Now*, *Strictly 4 My N.I.G.G.A.Z.*, and *Me Against the World*, sold millions of copies. But despite his commercial success, trouble always stalked Tupac. In 1995, Tupac went to prison following his conviction for a 1993 sexual-assault charge. Almost overnight, the Hip-Hop star found himself alone and friendless, in a scary place to be—serving time in the cold and impersonal walls of Clinton Correctional Facility in Dannemora, New York.

In years past, Suge Knight had tried to lure Tupac away from Interscope, the label he was signed to for his first three albums, but Tupac had always refused. After three hit albums and a good income from the label, why change? Things were different once he was serving time. Executives and managers from the California-based Interscope Records did precious little for Tupac while he was behind bars. The trip out to New York was long, and cold, cloudy, and gritty Dannemora was hardly a tourist destination. There were other artists to care for at Interscope, so Tupac fell off the plate. There are few kinds of pain like neglect, and Suge was there to swoop in to take advantage.

Unlike the executives at Interscope and even most of Tupac's friends, Suge flew out to visit the Hip-Hop icon regularly. The meetings revealed that, in addition to the neglect that Tupac felt, he needed to raise $1.4 million in bail in order to get out while he appealed his conviction. Suge had found the pain that he and Death Row Records could fix to sign one of the biggest hits in Gangsta Rap.

After raising $250,000 and arranging for MCA and Interscope to cover the rest, Suge secured Tupac's freedom and a three-album contract with the artist.[5] That deal allowed Tupac to make *All Eyez on Me*, his last and most successful album, with 10 million copies sold. That's a pretty good outcome for poking around to find and eliminate a client's pain. But even though this example of the hustler's game is totally boss, it glosses over the hard work associated with the critical follow-up tasks in sales: negotiating and closing.

Once a salesperson has an "in" with a customer, there are still a few steps before revenue starts raining. Negotiating and closing involves setting conditions, prices, and final agreement. Customers will vary on the importance they place on any particular element of the sale. To deal with that variability, the sales representative has to know the limits of a good deal and have the flexibility to work through the back-and-forth with the client to get to the end.

Let's start with the limits of a good deal. A salesperson needs to know how much authority they have to modify terms of an agreement. A good organization will give its sales force guidelines to inform them of the minimum revenue or benefits required for a deal to be profitable and the flexibility to make some concessions during negotiations. The idea behind this is that an uninformed salesperson could give away the store if the deal costs the company too much money or carries with it impossible obligations in terms of logistics and quality. The guidelines should inform the sales team where their authority ends and when to call in higher-ups for final decision-making.

Sales are many things, but they are not one-size-fits-all. Maybe some businesses are successful with a single sales methodology, but there aren't many like that. The needs and wants of each customer are different, and a good sales plan takes that into account. The salesperson needs flexibility in negotiating to make sure that the company doesn't lose sales due to needlessly rigid terms of payment, warranty and service support, delivery, or some other factor important to the customer. Sales-terms flexibility makes the customer feel that they have been cared for and treated special, and who doesn't like to feel special?

Live Nation Entertainment is a multibillion-dollar event-coordinating super-giant. Regardless of what genre of music you're into—Rock, R&B, Techno, Country, Hip-Hop, or even Scottish Pirate Metal (yes, that's a thing)—if you've been to a concert at a major venue anywhere in North America or even in many places around the world, the chances are you are one of Live Nation's customers. The company makes its money organizing, promoting, and managing events. They connect entertainers with the logistical, promotional, and physical support necessary to execute mass gatherings like concerts in highly sought-after locations.

Having a ginormous piece of the event-coordination market, Live Nation's size allows it to flex muscle to get preferential terms for virtually everything: food services, security, rent on facilities, local promotional and marketing activities, and even the artistic talent that draws the crowd. If an artist wants to do a first-class concert tour, it is hard to escape Live Nation. Even though there are other options for event management, they don't compete well for size, scope, and reach. As a result, Live Nation offers entertainers a modest cut of the total revenue for serving as the centerpieces of the events. That is, unless you are Sean "Jay-Z" Carter.

In Hip-Hop, there was no act bigger than Jay-Z. His name alone could sell out 40,000 seats in a stadium in minutes. After having achieved near-godlike status, Jay-Z took about a three-year break from touring. As a multimillionaire many times over, he could afford the time off from the hassles of life on the road. But Jay decided in 2008 that he was willing to get back into the concert game, and his idea was a 62-show tour called Blueprint 3. The tour was projected to bring in about $60 million in ticket sales, a number large enough to make a hungry corporation's mouth water. Live Nation wanted Jay-Z. It was willing to modify its typical artist agreements giving

Jay-Z a much greater share of the total revenue. "Since signing with Live Nation, Jay-Z's average gross per concert is over $1 million—nearly twice as much as Lil Wayne, the next-most successful live rapper."[6]

The more famous Jay-Z became, the more clout he had to negotiate terms with event coordinators like Live Nation. Live Nation was willing to be flexible on terms, giving up some margin because it made more, much more, on the increased volume of ticket sales with Jay-Z as a headliner. It was just smart salesmanship.

No sale is truly complete without getting referrals for new sales. Once one sale is done, it is time to go get another one. It's a never-ending cycle. To help ease the process of finding new opportunities, wise businesspeople turn to their existing customers. Customer referrals are genius, because customers know their partners and competition, and they frequently buy similar products and services. Customers might not be in a hurry to see their supplier provide a good deal to the competition, but it is worth asking. Another advantage of referrals is for the warm introduction to a new sales prospect. As we've said before, folks are suspicious of salespeople, but a positive review and recommendation from an existing customer can really improve the likelihood for sales with the referred client. As such, companies should consider incentives for customers who provide referrals like gifts or one-time discounts. Business should be a two-way street with benefits.

Bling, the blinding, over-the-top jewelry and personal decoration, might have come into fashion without Hip-Hop, but Hip-Hop certainly gave bling a big boost. For rappers, emcees, producers, and DJs who want to look the part of a top-billing entertainer, bling is practically a prerequisite. Bejeweled pimp cups, full-fist rings, platinum grills, thick, back-spasm-inducing gold chains, and enough ice to give someone frostbite are all par for the course in Hip-Hop culture. The precious metals and stones are all outward demonstrations of material wealth, and Hip-Hop loves to show off.

Avianne Jewelers in Midtown Manhattan services the Hip-Hop set with a long list of decorative rings, necklaces, earrings, chains, cufflinks, bracelets, and pendants. The bling they offer is blinding. When Avianne attracted top-tier artists like Cam'ron and Nicki Minaj, they knew that they had an in with a key demographic. Since the Rap stars seemed to enjoy their product, the jewelers politely asked who else they might interest in some high-end celebrity glitter. As a result, Avianne has enjoyed steady sales because of the referrals, and Nicki and Cam'ron know that they can count on Avianne for a good deal on their bedazzling adornments down the road.

A Crime Family of Products: Complementary Creations

Marketing can identify customer needs, and, based on the research, companies may offer specifically tailored products and services to address initial requirements to get their foot in the door. A little more investigation might reveal that customers need complementary products and services that your company can offer without having to reach terribly far outside of the organization's comfort zone. We call these a family of products.

Think of online travel companies. Many of them, like Expedia and Travelocity, started their services focusing on airline ticket sales searching flight options from most major airlines. When these companies first appeared on the web, it was a revolution for the travel industry. Millions of people flocked to make purchases quickly and conveniently from the comfort of their homes and offices. The travel companies realized almost immediately that there were plenty of services above and beyond airline tickets: hotels, rental cars, and, to a lesser degree, restaurant reservations and tourist activities. These additional services rounded out the family of products that made the travel companies more relevant to the customers who wanted one-stop shopping. It was smart business. Hip-Hop has its own versions of product families: the artist crews.

Christopher George Smalls grew up in and represented Brooklyn, New York, in the 1970s and '80s. His stout appearance earned him his nickname, "Big," which would morph into his various stage names: "Biggie" and "The Notorious B.I.G." He had the pedigree typical of rappers at the time: poverty, limited success in education, and a desire for something better. Biggie simultaneously sold drugs and found an artistic outlet to express himself: Rap. After appearing in *The Source* in the Unsigned Hype section, P Diddy brought Smalls in to Uptown Records to cut an album.

> *What took Hip-Hop by storm with the debut of Notorious B.I.G. was his candid Rapping style, which operated much in the spirit of the drug trade he had come up in . . .* Ready to Die *was a perfectly rounded experience for any Hip-Hop listener. It covered all spectrums of the hustler psyche—from the ups of instant money, notoriety, and constant female and fan adulation to the downs of the stress that accompanies becoming an overnight sensation.*[7]

Ready to Die would go triple platinum, and it changed Biggie from a street hustler into a Hip-Hop sensation practically overnight. Once that happened, he used his star power to branch out. Biggie invited members of his old crew to be part of his new gig at Uptown, so he created the Junior Mafia, a collection of Little Caesar, Chico, Nino Brown, cousins Larceny and Trife, MC Klepto, and Lil' Kim, the female rapper who would become Biggie's love interest and protégé. You might not recognize all the names, but that is typical. Most of the Junior Mafia were second-tier artists.

By 1995 in Hip-Hop, it had become commonplace for a marquee Rap act like Biggie to put his posse on following his own initial success—Ice Cube had done it with Lynch Mob, Ice-T with the Rhyme Syndicate, Snoop Dogg with the Dogg Pound, Tupac with the Outlawz. Rappers like Biggie were usually featured in almost every song on the crew album, typically in the chorus or verse, or sometimes in both if it was a single, and most crew albums were expected to go gold, selling 500,000 copies. Additionally, most were released within range of the star rapper's initial blow-up in popularity to provide maximum exposure and capitalize on the lead MC's success in selling his crew.[8]

The employment of second-tier artists was a good deal for everyone involved. Tier-two artists got, at the very least, the opportunity for fame and fortune in their own right, which they wouldn't have had without the support of a headliner like Biggie.[9] The record company sold additional albums, and fans got to see top-billing stars in a variety of musical settings. Family can be a good thing in life and in sales.

Enbiggen the Market: Widening Sales Opportunities

If a family of products helps sell new goods and services to existing customers (and others), taking existing products to a wider market is another useful sales technique. Companies divide markets into different parts as a tool to correctly target customers since one-size-fits-all sales are generally ineffective. While market segments may be different from one another in a variety of ways, it is possible to still sell the same product to many if not all of them.

Take peanut butter for example. The sticky, protein-rich gooeyness is famous as filling for kids' sandwiches, as a long-distance hiking diet staple, and as a surprisingly effective, improvised shaving cream. Given its deliciousness, peanut butter appeals to a wide swath of the North American market, but that wide swath of the market does not buy their product in the same store. High-end customers want to be wooed with brand names and exclusive and expensive grocery stores. More cost-conscious consumers are content to buy generic or store-brand peanut butter. How does a business bridge that marketing divide? Three words: private-label manufacturers. These manufacturers fill a sort of generic product for stores *and* make up branded peanut butter companies' capacity shortfalls. In many cases, the difference between the generic and branded products is negligible. Only the packaging and retail point of sale change. Private-label manufacturers are able to sell the same product to nearly the whole market.

Despite the genre's good qualities, radio managers in the 1980s and early 1990s had a hard time seeing how anyone could sell Rap music outside the Black community. It was a world before "fusion" swept the culinary scene and food trucks descended upon a public dying for such diverse food choices as fugu, slices of the deadly poisonous Japanese puffer fish, or fried Twinkies, the answer to the unasked question on how to make a Twinkie even less nutritious. At the time, commercial leaders in entertainment tended to view the world rather monochromatically. Never mind the lessons previously taught about cross-market sales from Jazz, Blues, R&B, Rock, and Disco. In the minds of the musical-distribution hierarchy, Hip-Hop would not break the color barrier. Fortunately, there were young people with different ideas about the commercial viability of a hot new sound.

Bill Stephney was something of a Hip-Hop marketing specialist. As a musician, his passion for music opened the door for him to appreciate Rap early in the genre's development. Stephney wrote articles about Hip-Hop while in college, and he parlayed his interest into a radio show in New York, Rap's birthplace and developmental laboratory. However, he found even New York's radio stations reluctant to take a chance on Hip-Hop. As stated earlier, managers couldn't see how the new sound could break out of the ghetto. Stephney decided that he would change the way that program directors and station managers would think about music by redefining it in commercial terms.

> *Stephney understood that radio stations on both sides of the racial divide were on a new kick of courting adults. It wasn't because kids weren't a lucrative market. It was just that radio programmers simply didn't have the knowledge or the stomach to play the music that kids wanted to hear. Black stations, Stephney thought, could slaughter the pop outlets if they just marketed Black music, including Rap, to a young White audience. Kind of like selling pizza: It's Italian food, but you don't just sell it to Italians.*[10]
>
> *. . . Stephney . . . felt that Hip-Hop should be marketed not as Black music, but as teen music, a station like Hot 97 was the perfect place to start.*[11]

Hot 97 was looking to expand its market share. The Latin music that it played at the time had given the station as much growth as it was going to get. The musical mix, including Hip-Hop, that Stephney was proposing seemed to be a good way to shake up the market. Hot 97 did pick up new teen listeners from across the racial divide as a result of the change, making it one of the most popular stations at the time, and the revenue from added advertising sales helped the bottom line. Good things can come from strategic sales of a product to a wider market.

Posting Up: Selecting Sales Locations

Reaching the customer can be a question of marketing, but it is also a question of logistics. How does a business attract its clientele? In accordance with the first rule of real estate, location has a lot to do with it. Business locations need to meet the tastes and convenience of the customer and still give logistical benefits to the company in the form of easy support or sustainable costs.

If you've listened to his music, you know that New York rapper Biggie Smalls sold drugs; and when it came to locations to do the job, he chose wisely both for his customers' convenience and his own need for security. He identified his primary corner for operation as Fulton Street and Washington in Brooklyn.[12] While Biggie's spot didn't have the panache or steady stream of wealthy patrons of Fifth Avenue and 59th Street at the south end of Central Park, his chosen place of business had distinct advantages that contributed to the success of his business.

The location made sense for Biggie and his customers. Washington is one of the few continuous two-way traffic streets in an area full of narrow, stop-and-go, one-way, north-south streets. Fulton is a four-lane, east-west cross street one block south of medium-use Gates Avenue, about one block north of the busier Atlantic Avenue, providing customers convenient access by car to come and go with ease or the option of using one of two bus routes. The neighborhood was a typical Brooklyn mix of residential- and commercial-use buildings.

A dealer could post up at the intersection and not be overexposed to police based on the relatively high volume of foot traffic, and the foot traffic in turn attracted regulars and impulse buyers alike. In the event that the cops did move in, the dealers and customers had their choice of exit directions with plenty of cover to make a relatively clean getaway. Traffic and buzz worked

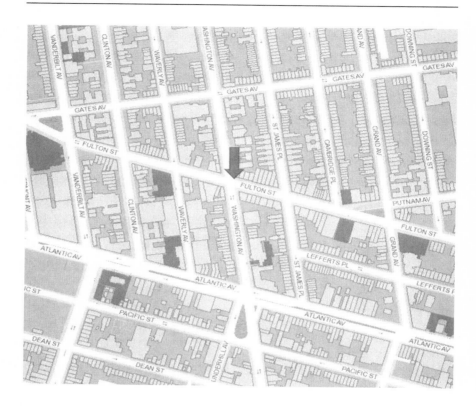

in his favor, too. Biggie's carefully sited dealer's spot ensured that he did not have to rely on mere word-of-mouth marketing to grow his sales. He didn't overpay for the location since, as a public space, it was effectively free.[13]

If Biggie did well siting his point of sale, the same cannot be said for Albert "Prodigy" Johnson of Mobb Deep and his clothing store, Infamous. He managed to locate his store in a terrible location *and* overspend on it. Prodigy came up with his "me-too" fashion idea after hitting a rough patch with Havoc, his musical partner, and after seeing the Wu-Tang Clan rake in $11 million from Wu-Wear within a few short years.[14] Having first looked at a more upscale location in Queens for $10,000 a month in rent, Prodigy instead picked a "gutted-out, empty storefront" at 132nd Street and Eighth Avenue in Harlem for $2,000 a month.

While he deserves some credit for having considered his overhead costs, he lost points for not understanding his business and the importance of a high-quality location for it.[15]

Prodigy could not replicate the wild success of Wu-Wear by picking a third-rate location for Infamous. Unlike the higher risks that customers of illicit drugs were willing to take to visit Biggie in Brooklyn, many Wu-Wear customers shopping for edgy Hip-Hop clothes did not want to fight their way uptown to Harlem for Infamous T-shirts. They did not want to schlep blocks and blocks from the nearest subway station or fight for the limited parking available around the store all to go to a spot where two men had been shot and one man killed shortly before the store's grand opening. To put an exclamation point on Prodigy's poor location decision-making, he closed the store down within a month of opening the doors.[16]

The Interweb Grind: Online Sales

Online presence or virtual marketplaces are somewhat more difficult. On the World Wide Web, it is a challenge to replicate the traffic equivalent of Biggie's site at Washington and Fulton. Building an online presence can be a lot of work. There are a few things to consider for a business's online presence: who the customers are and how to attract them, site setup, and how to manage payment and logistics.

A big part of successful online sales is knowing who your customers are so that you can attract them to your sites via links in articles, videos, and advertising in web locations they are likely to visit. There are plenty of marketing firms that can help a company find its customers online once you know who they are. Here we are talking about companies like Portent Inc., Mainstreethost, Full Media, or, to a certain degree, even Facebook and Google. They buy the results from others or actually track consumers in their navigation of the web using cookies, search results, IP address matching, and a long list of other terrifying cyber-stalker tactics yet commercially useful techniques. The result is that a business can deploy advertisements and strategic links back to a website to generate sales activities.

For Def Jam Recordings to be successful, Russell Simmons had to know who was actually buying his product so that he could target them more effectively. Unlike too many other marketing firms, Simmons saw diversity as a natural result of the wide appeal of Hip-Hop music.

> *We know that roughly 45 million people worldwide spend $12 billion annually on Hip-Hop products. And don't think it's just Black folks I'm talking about. When I worked at Def Jam, the RIAA figured out that 80 percent of the people who bought our records were non-African American. That's why I laugh every time I get called an African-American mogul.*[17]

Using the RIAA marketing data to recognize who Hip-Hop customers were and where to find them allowed Def Jam to target advertising appropriately around the United States. While this might not have been necessary with big-name acts whose buzz would take on a life of its own, it was especially helpful to promote second-tier acts who needed a bigger push to capture sales.

Another element is structuring your online presence in a functional, user-friendly way. Whether your company blankets every possible online outlet with a presence on Facebook, Twitter, LinkedIn, and Yelp, or it has just a single website, the utility of your pages has an outsized effect on sales activities. Make it attractive and easy to use, and customers will favor it over the competition. If it is poorly formatted for various devices or navigates badly, don't expect visitors to stick around. If you or your team don't know how to design and build sites, don't worry. There is a whole industry for that. A quick search for design-build companies or pre-fab websites will blow up all over your screen.

Rappers use their social media accounts similarly to the way businesses do to get and keep attention. They go for eye-catching graphics. They stock the content with entertainment, "fan food," if you will. Since top-tier, marquee artists are frequently unschooled or simply lack the time to manage their sites, they outsource the responsibilities to media teams to keep up posts, adjust content, and even find new ways to monetize the fan base by promoting various products for commissions and kickbacks. The next time you get spammed with pop-up ads following your favorite Hip-Hop entertainer, you'll know why.

If your organization is online, its purpose is to drum up business. Although there are companies that don't do direct sales online, managing payments and service logistics is a vital function. There are plenty of headaches that can go along with managing customer expenditures online, but there is plenty of upside. If your organization can deal with the security concerns of processing payments, there is relatively quick money to be made. If not, there are always third-party payment-processing companies like PayPal who will manage that aspect of the operations for a fee.

Getting the product to the end user is really what the customer cares about. Shipping logistics can be a challenge for initial deliveries and returns, so businesses need to spend time on logistical matters. You can let the carrier determine shipping costs rather than try to figure out the exact rates yourself for every transaction. Then again, if you can afford it, customers love free shipping. Product and service delivery should be as easy for your clients as a company can afford.

The Source, Hip-Hop's flagship publication, featuring extensive articles on artists, politics, and fashion started as little more than a one-page flyer. David Mays, the founder, had "sold four ads for $65 apiece . . . Local shops took reams of the newsletter for their Rap-curious customers, and Mays sent *The Source* to record companies around the country . . ."[18] Postage for the increasingly lengthy journal was not insignificant, but Mays and others at the growing publication felt that they needed to absorb a certain amount of distribution pain in order to establish a foothold with radio stations, record stores, and labels before they could divert costs exclusively to customers and advertisers. *The Source* today bears little resemblance to the scrappy flier from back in the day, and a smart policy on shipping costs at its inception probably had a lot to do with its success.

RUN THIS TOWN: MANAGEMENT FUNDAMENTALS

"LIKE A BOSS" FROM THE COMEDY TRIO Lonely Island is a killer song title. I couldn't have paid for a more appropriately titled Hip-Hop single for a chapter on management and leadership. Then I actually listened to it as part of the research for this book. The hope that I'd had to be able to tie in the leadership themes of a Rap song were dashed before I even made it to the second verse. While the mention of leading a workshop, remembering people's birthdays, and directing workflows was a great start, the tune's subsequent content was not a particularly inspiring lesson in business administration. From the part about hitting on subordinates and micromanaging staff through to the part about performing lewd acts and ultimately crashing into the sun, I realized that I might have to go elsewhere for Hip-Hop content to teach the lessons of management and leadership. Screw you, Lonely Island. You failed me.

Never fear, though, loyal reader. After all of the knowledge you'll get out of this, you'll be able to lead a team like a slightly different, definitely better, boss.

Leadership involves the relationship between a mission and people. Good leaders find ways to get people to do work well.

Bad ones usually piss off the people and frequently fail to achieve even their most superficial goals. Entrepreneurs, executives, and managers must be able to communicate with the people and organizations that will do the work. Following the rules of working smarter and not harder, the head of a group is responsible for the technical competence of the people and seeking opportunities for innovation. To address the human component of leadership, those in charge have to address the needs and wants of their employees and create motivational programs that keep people performing.

Over and above the things that motivate individuals, culture shapes how an entire organization treats its people, its customers, and its suppliers, and how well it faces a changing world. Managerial decision-making provides guidelines for leaders in the various environments they face, and then there is how to recover from mistakes at work when they inevitably happen. Managers have to deal with emotions and stress, both their own and others', in order to maintain a healthy atmosphere.

You Used to Call Me on My Cell Phone: Communications at Work

Most frustrations at work and many Hindenburg-style commercial catastrophes have resulted from poor communication. For that reason, managers have a greater responsibility than others for clear and complete exchange of information in and outside of the organization. The intent behind good communication is to engage and inform superiors, subordinates, peers, customers, suppliers, and anyone else in the business environment. The better connected and engaged people feel, the more easily work goes; and the lower the chances of commercial failure, dissatisfied customers, or torqued-off employees murdering their corporate officers. Leaders need to know how to use the right tools, explain why, pay attention, and ask questions to accomplish that.

Emoticon-only texts, passive-aggressive notes on the walls in the breakroom, Facebook termination notices, and the most reviled of all of them, the mass e-mail-to-all, are about the worst ways to connect in business. Using the right communication formats and tools makes a huge difference in how well recipients receive and respond to information, so a boss should consider means and audiences when speaking, writing, calling, or about to hit the "Send" button on a message.

The seriousness of a message may drive the method in which it gets delivered. Let me give you some examples. Judges don't text the jury's guilty verdicts to defendants. Doctors (hopefully) don't deliver terrifying test results to a patient's voicemail; and Bloomingdale's ought not to have encouraged date rape through a public advertising campaign to "spike your best friend's eggnog when they're not looking." Some messages just have got to be delivered in person . . . well, don't even use in-person communication to promote drugging and date rape. It's a good bet that will come back to haunt you.

Serious messages usually call for direct contact—face-to-face if possible, or video or teleconference if it isn't. They require emotionally understanding connection that is difficult to achieve in any other format except direct, person-to-person interactions. The non-verbal communications that come with this style can add authenticity and meaning in a way that less direct means can't. Interacting directly with people affords everyone the opportunity to respond dynamically to the information being presented, which, with serious subjects, should be handled delicately for best results. And if results are what you're looking for, check out this case study in communication.

According to urban legend, when Suge Knight wanted Dr. Dre out of his contract with Eazy-E's Ruthless Records so that he could help found Death Row Records, Suge didn't ask Eazy via fax, e-mail, or certified mail. Instead, he preferred the hands-on touch you get only with hired goons and death threats against friends and family. Entering the recording studios where Eazy was one evening, Suge and his posse used a series of less-than-professional methods to get Eazy to sign Dre's release.[1] Depending on who is telling the story, Eazy was punched, kicked, clubbed, intimidated, and/or dangled off an upper-floor balcony. See? When you need gravitas in your professional communications, face-to-face is the way to go.

More routine or mundane messages can afford to go out over more expeditious and impersonal channels like text, e-mail, fax, and/or the long list of social media options. Yes, virtually all options are on the table for lighter subjects, but all communications ought to be professional. Take the time to do spell- and grammar-check. Make sure that the correct people are included (or appropriately excluded), and scrub the message content to make sure that it doesn't have any embarrassing material before you hit "Send." Failing to do these things increases the chances that a note will have errors, omissions, or other awkward elements that will distract from whatever the message was intended to be.

Managers can score bonus points using the recipient's preferred means of communication. It is hard to get people's attention under the best of circumstances, so using a mode of transmission to which your audience is favorably disposed improves the odds that your message gets through. This is where you employ all of the skills from your sociology, anthropology, and communications classes to identify auditory, visual, and tactile/kinesthetic learning styles. Throw in your personal knowledge of individuals and their favorite communication channel like text, e-mail, phone, etc., and the chances the recipients will get your message go up. If you can mix and match your message media to square with your recipients, you'll be balling.

Hip-Hop is in part a means of communicating. The music, the fashion, and cultural elements are all forms of expression meant to reach people . . . and generate billions of dollars a year in sales, and that is a kind of communication, too . . . Hip-Hop has adapted over time to maintain and increase its relevance to its fans with macro and micro trends. New styles pop up, and old ones fade away into only the most-obscure-hipster playlists. Popular trends in music like southern Hip-Hop (the "party music, full of hypnotic hooks and sing-along choruses that get the ladies on the dance floor"[2]) grabbed a generation of fans less interested in the heavy lyrics of New York Rap. With 30 songs of *Billboard's* Top 40 belonging to southern rappers in 2009, that is effective communication.[3] Hip-Hop is also capable of more nuanced connections with small groups or even individuals with vibrant local music scenes, lesser-known, but talented bands, and even local fashion trends. If business leaders can be as adaptable and successful as Hip-Hop at connecting with people and communicating messages, there is plenty of money to be made.

Communications at work have an all-too-common cause for breakdown: the failure to explain "why." People want to believe that their lives have meaning, so giving people good, honest explanations for the work they do improves morale or at least limits the emotional downside some jobs can carry. Don't get me wrong. This is a tough part of business communication. However, if you can't explain why you're doing something, a policy changed, hours are long, or a decision went the way it did, that should trigger a larger examination of operations.

Aubry Drake Graham, a.k.a "Drake," was a Canadian Hip-Hop sensation who blew up the scene with hits like "One Dance," "Best I Ever Had," "Hot Bling," and "Hold On, We're Going Home." He launched himself into the top tier of Hip-Hop celebrities after earning multi-platinum status on four studio albums, won swarms of awards, and dominated the charts like few others. That is an objective commercial success; and the labels that signed him, like OVO Sound, Young Money, Cash

Money, Republic, Aspire, Universal Motown, and Boy Better Know, all benefited financially from backing the star. But there were others who had the opportunity to get a piece of the Drake action and missed out.

Aliaume Damala Dara Akon Thiam, better known by his stage name Akon, founded Konvict Muzik in 2005, near the height of his success. At one point in time, the label had some fair Hip-Hop talent on the roster with Faheem "T-Pain" Najm being the most prominent. After a number of successful album releases from the label, Kardinal Offishall brought Akon the recordings of a relatively unknown Canadian artist, none other than Drake. Akon passed on the opportunity to sign him.

Konvict Muzik has not had much success since then. Years into the economic doldrums, employees of the label who joined the company believing that they might be the next Death Row, Uptown, Cash Money, or Interscope Entertainment wanted to know why things hadn't turn out the way they had hoped. As the head of the organization, Akon had the unpleasant job of explaining how Konvict Muzic allowed Drake, whose success would have changed the fortunes of the label, to slip through their fingers. "I honestly did pass on him because at the time, he didn't sound like what he sounds like today . . . 'The Best I Ever Had'—it wasn't even close to what that sounded like."[4]

That explanation might be cold comfort for the employees and artists at Konvict Muzic who wished for greater success for the label, but Akon deserves credit for explaining his decision to pass on the man who would become one of Hip-Hop's brightest stars. The honesty gives Konvict personnel a window into the A&R decision-making process, and one could hope that Akon finds the next musical sensation since he obviously regrets his error.

Communications are a two-way street. It is more than successful transmission of information. There is also listening for replies, and that means paying attention and asking questions. There are at least two reasons for this:

1. You never know when someone is going to have a brilliant idea or a problem that needs attention.
2. Teams work better when members feel that leadership hears their voices.

Listening to your people and soliciting feedback is a proactive step for managers to engage team members that generally costs very little but has a huge upside if handled right. That means focusing on the person in front of you, avoiding the tempting distraction of your nearest electronic device, and maybe even making eye contact if you can manage it. When asking questions, you'll get bonus points if you can phrase them in a way that gets more than yes/no answers, and a good technique to do that is to use questions that include who, what, when, where, why, and how. Oh, and if you are the talkative type, leave a long enough pause for a shy person to formulate a response. The pause in conversation shows a commitment to listen to the other person and gives them time to think.

As a manager, you're held to a higher standard than others, and that puts some limits on what you can or should communicate with your people. Unfortunately, that means applying a personal filter. Griping to subordinates is unprofessional and counterproductive. Not every thought or opinion deserves to be shared and certainly not with the whole staff.

Wired magazine, the technology and culture publication, was always looking for ways to keep people clicking on its sites. Getting O'Shea "Ice Cube" Jackson, one of the pillars of the Gangsta Rap institution N.W.A., to do a Google Autocomplete Interview provided *Wired* some good click bait and gave Ice Cube a chance to answer fan queries. The interview was a compilation of the Internet's most frequently asked questions about the rap-per; and whenever someone compiles the Internet's most common searches, there is always going to be some eye-roll-worthy material. Still, Cube showed patience with *Wired*'s interview gimmick and made a pretty entertaining video. Maybe it was a little cheesy, but Cube's effort connected with people. If he can put himself out there, a decent manager can do the same for their team members.

Innovention: Working Smarter, Not Harder

Leadership doesn't begin and end with grand visions, the ability to communicate, or even the knack for motivating people. Knowing how to do the job and seeking better ways of doing it are also a leader's responsibilities. Bosses must look at the skills and abilities of the team members and empower them to innovate to improve operations. These are hallmarks of great organizations because they smooth out processes and add value in different areas. Innovation might not come in a can, but there are things that companies can do to open the doors to innovation. Employee training and process improvement are ordinary and relatively easy enabling factors to make a company run better. Every business has to decide how much time and effort can be spent on them, but the benefits are there for those who make the investment.

It is hard to overestimate the importance of a well-trained workforce. Their abilities allow them to handle everyday assignments effortlessly, providing them with the time and energy to address the unpredictable problems that businesses face, like market or technology disruptions. They can solve problems for customers, making their experience better, and there are morale benefits for companies that invest in people.

Workplace training varies tremendously, and deciding who needs what kind of instruction is challenging. Anyone who doesn't believe that must not be aware of society's never-ending debate about education. Costs, time, resources, and results always have trade-offs for the organization, but leaders can find a balance in their training plans. A low-cost option is for management to coordinate courses internally, relying on veteran employees to teach new personnel. However, if a business needs new skills and abilities, trade associations, educational institutions, and private companies have generalized and industry-specific training programs that can meet at least some requirements for most companies. Employees will return from these events having been exposed to new ideas, people, and ways of doing business. That investment in worker development may be the key to boosting employee empowerment, perfecting operations at the company, or even upsetting the whole industry with new initiatives.

Back in Queens in the 1980s and '90s, lots of local industries had workplace training and third-party innovation-consulting services available for things like accounting, logistics, and manufacturing. The same could not be said for the drug trade. If you were new to the trade, you were going to have to get your training from veteran dealers. Unlike the snorrendous PowerPoint presentations, lame handouts, and prehistoric instructional videos many companies inflict upon employees as part of an onboarding process, the OJT that 50 Cent got was hella engaging and immediately relevant.

50's mentor, Brian, broke down the cocaine-to-crack drug-conversion process into the sort of individual steps that could have fit in easily on the stoner-friendly *Bob Ross: Joy of Painting* show. He explained the components he would need, their costs, and where 50 could buy them. They were things like "capsules and Gem Blue Star razor blades to cut the rocks," which he could get at the local bodega.[5] Brian even showed him how to cook materials with the proper ratios (two parts cocaine, one part baking soda) for crack. All training needs to be measured by how effective it was, and Brian must have been a great instructor. "By my second time at the stove, I could create a perfect mixture by eye—no measuring, no nothing. I was like, 'It can't be this fuckin' easy.'"[6] Mad props, Brian. Any occupational educator would be proud of those results. Well, maybe if it wasn't a felony . . .

At their core, modernization and improvement efforts challenge assumptions in the business. Innovation can reduce costs or generate new revenue streams with the intent to benefit the company, employees, or customers. Given their position and authority, managers need to keep this on their assignment list, but it should be a shared responsibility with the whole organization, since original ideas can come literally from anywhere. Extremely well-run companies are able to set aside personnel, time, and resources specifically for innovation. Think of Google's cushy, imagination-expanding nap pods or Microsoft's high-end collaboration spaces, and you get a sense of the money a corporation might be willing to spend to make innovation possible. While that's cool, most advances in commercial activities come out of more ordinary environments. The conditions for innovation really require only the willingness of leadership to listen to ideas, try new things, and accept failure as an inevitable part of the process.

The people involved in modernization programs must be open to questioning assumptions about the company and how it does business. Leaders need to allow the free expression of ideas during discussions to get the widest range of innovation proposals, research topics, and data-collection targets possible. Following these brainstorming sessions, the group can eliminate impractical solutions; but, at the beginning, unrestricted communication is key to the ideas that can change things for the better. Once the team has narrowed down the list of plans, leadership needs to be willing to test them, and this is harder than it sounds. Organizations frequently suffer from the this-is-how-we've-always-done-it inertia, and only with the diplomatic-but-forceful effort of managers can anything ever change. Lastly, leaders have to be strong enough to accept the inevitable failures of improvement programs as the cost of doing business. Failures in innovation should not be punished. They are par for the course.

Let's return to our previous Hip-Hop business lesson. Sure, Brian was a good trainer, but what about management's responsibility for innovation? Good question. As it turns out, there was low-hanging fruit when it came to process improvements. Unlike delicious, store-bought cake mix, cooking crack does not result in an entirely useable product. Once the water, baking soda, and cocaine are mixed and heated in a container, the baking soda separates into sodium carbonate and carbon dioxide. These react with the hydrochloride in the cocaine, leaving a cocaine alkaloid compound that is sucked off to set and dry to make the rock. Without further intervention, the remainder of materials would result in scrap. Crack cooks, like any group of pioneering entrepreneurs, hated waste. 50 Cent's mentor, Brian, looked at the slurry and saw opportunity.

> *More important, [Brian] showed me how to take the runoff from the bottom of the pot and whip it into more crack. When I did that, it was like I was doubling my supply. I couldn't believe it.*[7]

Brian's discovery was a game-changer for him and his friends. He had arrived at that revelation though simple process improvements. He listened to other cooks talk about the financial pinch they felt from the slurry scrap. He had a trial-and-error approach to reprocessing the material until he found a method that rendered a saleable product. Although 50 Cent doesn't mention the failures, there were times during the scrap reprocessing experiment when the slurry had to be thrown away. There aren't many people good enough or lucky enough to hit a homerun on the first try. All businesses have opportunities to improve themselves, and leaders have a responsibility to encourage and direct those efforts.

Must Be the Money: Sources of Motivation

To address one of the human components of leadership, those in charge have to address the desires and needs of their employees and create incentive programs that keep people performing well. Compensation, personal recognition, and inspiration are three common levers of motivation. Leaders who know their people and find the right combination of incentives can get individuals and teams to move mountains.

Setting up fair compensation is essential to taking care of your people. Having cash and benefits provide people with the freedom to do the things they want outside of work, so it is no surprise that this is a strong motivational tool in the workplace. Different organizations compensate people differently, and, depending on your place in the organization, you may or may not have much control over how people are paid. However, for argument's sake, we'll look at a few of the options.

A raise in base salary is the centerpiece of compensation. For some folks, this is the yardstick of personal worth by which they measure themselves and others. Even if you aren't one of those types, most folks like having "walking-around money," and a little more jingle in their pockets never hurts. A boost to base salary or hourly wage increases an employee's taxable wages, and, consequently, they may receive more from Social Security in retirement. Some companies that offer 401(k) retirement programs allow employees to contribute a percentage of their earnings and may even make matching contributions. An increase in base salary in those circumstances would also entail an increase in the matching funds of the company to the employee's 401(k), essentially providing more free money to the lucky guy or girl getting the raise. Oh, and higher payroll taxes for the employer. Uncle Sam likes it when people get raises, too!

Figuring out how much an employee is "worth" in compensation terms is more of an art than a science. There are plenty of reliable, publicly available data sources that can give the upper and lower salary ranges for virtually any position by geographic region. Industry associations like the National Association of Manufacturers, American Bar Association, and Society of Professional Journalists put out employment statistics a few times a year. Just plug in the job title, location, and, occasionally, years of service, and out pops the average wage for your query. A manager's difficulty is figuring out if the salary range for an employee achieves the motivating function without breaking the bank.

Without casting any shade in saying so, Jay-Z is one of the most earnings-sensitive entertainers in Hip-Hop. And why not? As he states in Kanye West's "Diamonds from Sierra Leone," he is not a mere businessman. He is a business unto himself, a brand that must be nurtured and protected. Just as producers of high-end products refuse to offer their goods in discount stores for fear of cheapening the image, Jay-Z wouldn't walk across the street if the price weren't right, as many label executives, tour planners, merchandising promoters, and other entertainers learned the hard way in trying to contract him. In 2010, he made $63 million, more than twice the earnings of the next highest paid entertainer, P Diddy.[8] Those sorts of earnings do not happen accidentally.

Jay-Z's commercial success created a snowball effect with his earnings. *Reasonable Doubt* and *In My Lifetime* launched him on the path to stardom, which gave him the leverage to ask for increasingly higher payouts from record labels for subsequent work. And as long as he was delivering the goods, more and more money would roll in. If the entertainment industry wants Jay to work, they've got to be willing to pay the price. Of course, base salary isn't the only way to provide motivational recompense.

Bonuses are the easiest form of compensation increases. The flexibility of bonuses allows businesses to attract, reward, or keep employees without having to worry about the long-term costs of increases in base wages which compound over time and the associated payroll taxes on those higher earnings. They may be part of a recurring program like end-of-year bonuses, or they can be one-time, good-deal payouts for special occasions. Depending on your industry, there may be customary bonuses as part of the job, like finance and banking, which should be figured upfront. It is important to have rules on how and why bonuses are paid to let employees know when and how they can earn them and to prevent reward programs from being abused. Just like there are easy-to-access guidelines for salary ranges, there are plenty of bonus practices, formulas, and processes offered online like those listed on the website of the Society for Human Resources Management.

Artists' signing bonuses are the bedrock of the bling-bling stories in Hip-Hop. They are the big-dollar exclamation points that punctuate the change from street hustler to big-baller, from big-baller to Rap god, or from Hip-Hop hero back down to second-tier bench warmer. Clifford Joseph "T.I." Harris, part of the crowd of Atlanta rappers from the early 2000s, got his first signing bonus as an advance from Arista Records and LaFace Records for his first studio album, *I'm Serious*, which was based in a deal for $2 million.[9] It was a good deal for a high school dropout with a mixtape and a little bit of buzz. The two labels were looking to lock down the unsigned talent in the hopes of catching lightning in a bottle. But easy come, easy go. *I'm Serious* was a critical and commercial disaster. Sales slumped, with fewer than 200,000 copies sold, a poor showing for a freshman album. Fortunately for T.I. and the rest of the Hip-Hop nation, he pulled himself together and has released some killer albums over the years. Which brings us to another example: using a bonus to keep talent.

Dwayne "Lil Wayne" Carter was one of the youngest rappers to come out of New Orleans. Signed to Bryan "Birdman" Williams' Cash Money Records at age nine, he percolated with the label for years before he had his career breakout with a platinum hit, *Tha Block Is Hot*. Lil Wayne's image (including trademark dreadlocks), energy, and versatile artistic style took him places, commercially speaking, where few artists have ever gone before. On his first 11 studio albums, he earned six gold, three platinum, one double platinum, and one triple platinum record. By 2012, he had knocked Rock god Elvis Presley off of his long-held pedestal with the most songs on the *Billboard* Hot 100 chart. Williams and Cash Money had a superstar performer on their team, and Lil Wayne's more than 11 million copies sold made some serious bank for the label.

But companies cannot always count on employee loyalty without incentives, even when they practically raise them from diapers to adulthood. By the time he started to work on this twelfth album, Lil Wayne had been out in the world long enough to know that Cash Money was not the only show in town. His relations with Williams were far from perfect, with concerns about artistic freedom and financial mishandling. Like a lot of professionals in similar circumstances, Lil Wayne started to shop around for employment alternatives. Alarmed by the possibility of Wayne's departure and in an effort to keep their cash cow on the payroll, Cash Money offered a type of stay bonus with a $150 million, four-album contract. Just the advances from the deal would be enough to buy fleets of supercars, a subdivision of mansions, bling, and enough ink to cover the rest of Lil Wayne's already tattoo-crowded face and body.[10] While that kind of cash is tempting, when relations go sour, sometimes money isn't enough to maintain motivation.

All people want appreciation from others in their lives. There is an emotional high that goes with attention and praise. The need is so fundamental that examples of public recognition go back to the dawn of civilization. There were ornaments for the nobility, laurel wreaths for victors in the original Olympic Games, and military decorations for valor as far back as the Roman army. Beyond the individual's emotional need for them, honors have tremendous, positive effects by raising productivity, job satisfaction, and member loyalty when they are tied to the organization's goals, values, mission, and vision. Our desire for personal distinction and validation from our family, friends, coworkers, and even complete strangers make employee apperception and public recognition a must-do part of any leadership strategy.

The beauty of recognition as a motivational tool is its flexibility. From a simple "thank you" for a job well done through to elaborate imperial coronation ceremonies, leaders have a range of options to choose from when deciding how to acknowledge team members' superior performance. Good programs in the workplace cover parts of this spectrum. A personal "thank you" and "good work" costs nothing, but the benefits for some people can be more profound than large cash prizes or blinged-out trophies. More formal awards like employee of the month or salesperson of the year maintain a regularity that reduces the chances that a forgetful boss will fail to recognize employees over time. As with bonus systems, management should talk to employees about how selections are made for the recognition program. Companies can score points by seeking feedback from employees to ensure that it has the intended morale-boosting effects.

If you've ever watched music award shows, you can see that the Hip-Hop world appreciates great artistic efforts. There are the Grammies, MTV Video Music Awards, *Billboard* Music Awards, *The Source* Awards, and BET Hip-Hop Awards, just to name a few. They all center on common elements meant to pay appropriate respect to honorees, advance the art form, and give people a good show. The award selection process may vary from show to show from opaque and arbitrary (I'm looking at you, MTV VMA) to relatively open and honest. People within the industry understand the rules (or lack thereof) of each one. The shows themselves are broken into segments to honor the various musical categories and professional contributions to cover a wide swath of the industry for maximum participation. The artists, executives, and guests get decked out in their finest for the parade of entertainment activities from the pre-parties through the ceremony and on to the after-parties. The whole thing is enough to keep artists jazzed about their achievements, fans riveted by the spectacle, and caterers and event planners fat with cash. What more could anyone want from a recognition program?

Inspiration is perhaps the hardest method of motivation to pull off since it is more art than science. It is an emotion, and those are notoriously difficult to control. The art elements include a stew of conditions for the leader and the workers, including personal charisma, chemistry between individuals, and professional commitment. Leaders need to connect to the people on some level requiring regular, positive contact in the maintenance of the relationship. A leader has to believe (or at least make people think they believe) in what they are doing in order to get others to believe, too.

Most leaders know the science part of inspiration. There are common conditions that can help for this form of motivation. Inspired employees know where they are going, which relates directly back to how clear their mission and vision at work is and how well their leader connects them to the work. Inspired employees know how to do their job or have faith that someone will teach them. They feel free to try new things or collaborate with others. Additionally, the organization and the leader need to be consistent in performance. The breakdown of any one of these can defeat the motivational purpose.

People pick their favorite songs and artists in large part because of the emotions they evoke inside them. There were the euphoria-spawning dance Raps from the Dirty South, which shook the clubs. There was the cool-inducing, artistically experimental sounds of The Roots that made you think. And then there were the emotions that inspired people to action.

Compton, California, native Kendrick Lamar used his slow-rolling, politically conscious music to capture a large and loyal audience. Like the pioneers of 1990s Gangsta Rappers before him, Lamar devotes much of his music to chronicling the harsh realities of life on the street and in the neighborhoods: substance abuse, violence, racial injustice, and the need for something better in life. The themes in his songs evoke strong feelings, which probably accounts for his 3 million Instagram fans, 7 million Twitter followers, and 8 million Facebook likes. That's pretty respectable at a point in time when Hip-Hop's biggest commercial successes have not been long on civic-minded substance.

Lamar made charity a meaningful part of his public life. He gave away hundreds of thousands of dollars to music and after-school programs in his hometown. He supported the Red Cross, the homeless, and relief programs in India as part of his 2014 World Tour for Charity. Lamar embraced his role as a social activist and supporter of Black Lives Matter, encouraging others to push for social change. Fan forums are full of shout-outs of how Lamar and his music inspired them. Achieving the same effect at work probably doesn't require a society-changing political agenda or even two platinum records, but they couldn't hurt.

Damn, It Feels Good to Be a Gangsta: Culture at Work

Houston's favorite Hip-Hop sons, the Geto Boys, released a compilation album containing a song that captured the essence of organizational culture. Scarface, Bushwick Bill, Willie D, and Big Mike take turns singing the praises of their way of life in "Damn,

It Feels Good to Be a Gangsta." They trumpeted their core values of strength, cool, and excellence. The Geto Boys go into some of their accepted practices like dealing smart, judiciously using violence, and picking up women. They are proud of the sense of connection that comes with being part of their "in" group. The song expressed gangster ethos so perfectly that Mike Judge couldn't resist featuring it as an anthem for the underdog office drones in his cult classic movie, *Office Space*.

Everyone wants to feel good where they spend so much of their life, so it is hard to overvalue a good workplace culture. As the Geto Boys demonstrate, a culture is made up of an organization's core values, accepted practices, and its sense of connection, and they function like a garden when they are together. And like a garden, culture is a living thing that requires careful cultivation. Plants must get the attention they need to thrive, and weeds have to be rooted out. Culture is everyone's responsibility—management and staff alike.

A company's core values are not the platitudes that they ripped off from motivational posters and plastered around the walls. The core values are the things that *actually* get valued and prioritized. In good organizations, the propaganda in the frames on the walls is reflected in the high-quality support and attention that suppliers, customers, and employees receive. In bad ones, everyone knows that the real core values are about selfishness, laziness, and jealousy because they can see them in practice at work every day. Good core values don't guarantee success in business, but bad core values almost always catch up with companies in ugly ways like the Enron ethics and accounting scandal that crushed the company, the banking crisis that started the Great Recession, or the collapse of Death Row Records.

Time Inc. started *Vibe* magazine in 1993 to compete for the increasingly lucrative Rap music fan base against the Hip-Hop publication forerunner, *The Source. The Source* was started by Rap enthusiasts who loved the music and culture. On the other hand, *Vibe* was a corporate experiment, and it struggled for authenticity right from the start. Its core values were not universally shared between the staff of Hip-Hop reporters and Time's handpicked management, and their different understandings about what it meant to serve the Hip-Hop fan base would be a huge challenge.

The crisis came after a period of inconsistent monthly sales reports. The publication's young editor, Jonathan Van Meter, tried to put Madonna on the cover of the magazine in an effort to boost sales. The editorial crew, already upset by Van Meter's insistence on rigid office hours and corporate decorum, revolted. They were not putting a White pop star on the cover of a Hip-Hop magazine, when Spike Lee and Eddie Murphy were in the same issue. What kind of message did that send to the readers? "No matter how big Madonna was, no matter how many magazines she sold, she had no place on the cover of a magazine supposedly dedicated to Hip-Hop, a culture that determined its own superstars and icons."[11] In order to save the magazine, Van Meter recognized that he was part of the problem of core values, and he ultimately left *Vibe* for the good of the organization.

Accepted practices are the policies and activities that people do at work, from business hours and vacation policy to the quality of customer service and cleanliness of the bathrooms. All of these things say a lot about employee satisfaction and how engaged managers are. When things are going well, customers experience it with high-quality goods and services, employees take pride in their work, and the company will usually see its reward on the bottom line of the income statements. When they don't, well . . . there are plenty of examples of failed companies to tell that story. Business leaders are responsible for enforcing standards (even when it is uncomfortable) or accepting the blowback.

When Percy "Master P" Miller started No Limit Records in the Bay Area in the early 1990s, it was the Hip-Hop equivalent of a taco truck. But P was a workhorse. He signed artists, recorded and released their albums, and even tried some solo work of his own. Anyone who came to No Limit was expected to hustle to get their music out the door. That meant that artists and repertoire agents had to find new talent. Producers had to mix the music into a finished product. Artists had to record, perform, and promote their work. Everyone knew what Master P's expectations were, and they busted their humps to perform.

"P told MTV, 'When you got a fan base, feed that fan base. There's no such thing as too much music.' . . . Estimates for No Limit's profits are widely varied, but reports of sales in 1998, one of the label's peak years, are about $160 million."[12] There is only one way that a record label could go from zero to $160 million in sales in less than eight years, and that is with leadership and staff pulling together to make the sales happen. That is doing business right with accepted practices.

The sense of connection that employees have at work covers a lot of territory. It can be the laughter in the lunchroom or the brooding, *Game of Thrones*-style assassination plots hatched in dark places. Good connections do not require extravagant holiday parties, although those can be good. Instead, managers set the tone for interaction at work with their honesty, communication, and willingness to relate to people. The staff tends to work harder and more dependably in organizations where there is a high degree of honesty, clear communication, and an atmosphere that is safe to socialize in. A positive environment like that may be better than what they have outside of the job. If the situation is stifling and cold, it's a good bet that you'll find people watching the clock, phoning it in on projects, and making for the door as soon as they think they can get away with it. Why stay somewhere that sucks?

Although they were technically co-equals at Death Row Records, Dr. Dre let Suge control business decisions and the culture at the label, and that had a serious downside for everyone involved. Suge had strong opinions about how things were going to be. "To have a vision, and believe in something, you gonna work hard at it. When I had my vision with the music business, my whole motive was to work hard and be the best at it. So I treated it like we was a football team."[13]

Maybe that team atmosphere did exist at the beginning, but it didn't last long, in large part because of the way that Suge treated people. There was no sense of equality among the artists, with some getting much more attention than others. For many of them, albums were released late or not at all. There were shady finances, and even superstars like Tupac and Snoop felt like they were being shortchanged, as evidenced by their wage-theft lawsuits. There were the Bloods gang members prowling around the studios intimidating people. Dre, who technically had the authority to intervene, could only watch as artist after artist fled the poison culture at the label. There had been a sense of connection among employees at Death Row Records once, but Suge and his mismanagement went a long way to killing it. When Dre finally had had enough, he left, too.

Judgment Day: Managerial Decision-Making

Decision-making is another demanding aspect of the art of leadership, because everything at work involves a certain amount of choice about one thing or another. Whether they choose wisely or poorly, bosses generally have to do *something* . . . even if that means doing nothing. The circumstances of each day at work can be wildly different from one another, from the days so quiet that you might think there was tumbleweed blowing down the halls to hair-on-fire, end-of-the-world disasters. Managing a health club, running a photonics research lab, and overseeing musical programming for L.A.'s Power 106, the number one Hip-Hop station in the US, don't share many job-related tasks.

However, the amount, speed, and stress of activity could very easily be identical, and those are the most important factors in managerial decision-making.

Business authors David Snowden and Mary Boone spoke, in the *Harvard Business Review,* about the work environment and how it affects decision-making.[14] To paraphrase the writers, there are simple, complex, and chaotic settings. The differences between them change decision timing, information and resource availability, and opportunities for collaboration. Understanding the business environment and preparing to respond across a range of circumstances is how you "boss up" in your job.

In simple settings, routine reigns, and surprises are rare. Leaders and their staff are familiar with the stuff going on, and when something goes off the rails, they know how to get it back on the tracks. Even when they don't know how to fix it, they know the resources available to get the job done, like searching a database, running a report, or picking up the phone to maintenance. Under these circumstances, a good manager can and should consult the team or delegate tasks to knowledgeable employees. Consultation and delegation gives the staff a greater sense of ownership in the job and develops them for the future. It even provides opportunities to make the work more efficient, fun, better, faster, or cheaper. After all, in this setting, there isn't much upside to domineering and micromanaging. Deciding things in a simple environment can be easy, and your nice-guy boss suit fits great in these circumstances.

What could be more simple (and inevitable) than death? Despite improvements in healthcare, human mortality rates are still running at 100%, and that makes for some steady business of grieving families contacting the funeral homes. The staff schedules the ceremonies. Technicians prepare the bodies for eternal rest, and (barring the reanimation of flesh-eating corpses) it is wash, rinse, repeat for the business. While mortuary services have their own challenges, complex decision-making is not what the industry is famous for.

Complex settings involve uncertainties and moving parts. The right answer to a problem does not jump off the page, and there is no easy button to hit to make things better. Past experience and routines may not apply, which means that a manager has to rely on incomplete information, non-traditional data sources, and outside experts to come up with solutions. Taking too long to gather and analyze data is risky, but there are hazards to going off half-cocked. Decision-making in these situations frequently boils down to knowing the risks involved with different choices and deciding which one fits best with the company's priorities.

Think of the emergency that record companies experienced as album sales collapsed at the start of the Internet file-sharing trend. No one in the industry at the time had seen anything like it before. The financial toll was quick and devastating. Album sales dropped by 53 percent from $14.3 billion in 1999 to $7 billion in 2013.[15] The crisis involved intellectual property laws, global piracy, radical changes in product distribution, and shrinking profit margins; and everyone from newly-signed Hip-Hop artists to label executives took a bath in the economic losses.

Not willing to quietly take a fiscal beating, artists, attorneys, executives, entrepreneurs, and many others worked to create the legal and logistical framework of the music service environment that exists now. The Recording Industry Association of America (the same group that represents the music industry and certifies albums as gold, platinum, etc.) sued Napster, the poster child for file-sharing organizations. Seeing Napster's trouble and recognizing an opportunity, Apple created iTunes as a relatively inexpensive, legal, and tremendously profitable online music clearinghouse to benefit record companies and fans. YouTube marketed itself as the Internet's capital for user-driven video content. Each group assessed its risks resulting from lower album sales, and they explored the different technological and legal tools to respond to the threat. In some cases, they acted alone, and, in other cases, they acted collectively, like the RIAA suit. Although the final chapter in music distribution hasn't been written yet, the survivors learned about complex decision-making.

Chaotic settings tend to be high speed and very dynamic. The cause of a problem and its solution may or may not be clear. The leader's goal is to act to create order by controlling a few aspects of the situation. There is little or no time to debate courses of action, so communication from the top can be curt and directive. A manager can't be blamed for relying on some level of instincts under the circumstances. The thought processes in chaotic scenarios can be partially improved with some fire drill-style planning and well-organized, quick-reference materials since the drills and references can save critical time. Even so, there is no guarantee that the procedures or documents prepared for unprecedented emergencies will be useful in the clutch.

Between his time in the Army and becoming a Gangsta Rap superstar, Ice-T was into the robbery game. Unlike mortuary services, robbing high-end retail establishments tended to have complex and even chaotic decision settings. Although he prided himself on carefully planning his heists by casing his targets and preparing getaway routes, that wasn't enough one hot September night. Ice-T and his gang plotted to hit an Asian boutique specializing in designer clothes. However, despite the strategizing and prior experience, after just a few minutes inside the deserted store, a black-clad, armed guard surprised them.

That is when the job transitioned from merely complex to totally chaotic. As the guard started shooting at Ice-T and his crew, there wasn't time to review notes and no chance to huddle the gang for a brainstorming session. He did what leaders who thrive in chaos do. He pushed his crew out the door, jumped through the open window of his getaway car, and gave good, easy-to-follow advice: "Drive, muthafucka, drive!"[16] When the crisis was over and everyone was free and clear, they could laugh about their little adventure. They lived to rob another day.

You're Doing It Wrong: Mistakes at Work

Nobody's perfect . . . business leaders least of all. From little things like the 2008 mortgage-default-fueled banking crisis to total, world-shaking cataclysms like running out of coffee, stuff at work doesn't always go as planned. Assuming you didn't intentionally sabotage your company's operations, knowing how to bounce back from mistakes is as essential a business survival skill as basic literacy, eighth-grade math, or Brazilian jujitsu. The art of mistake recovery has a million aspects to it, but we'll focus on three that can get you started on your lifelong journey of trial and error in business. They are recognizing mistakes, correcting errors, and owning up to the slip-up.

Before you can do anything else, you've got to identify and understand the source of the error. When it comes to the root causes of mistakes, your ignorance, silent subordinates who know better, unengaged bosses, and pissed-off but passive-aggressive customers are the enemy. If you don't realize that you've screwed up, there is nothing to stop you from doing it again.

Proper mistake responses just reinforce the importance of open and honest communication. If the corporate culture is any good, you'll get more than one chance to recover from less-than-career-ending business blunders. Once you realize you've slipped up, you've got to understand how it happened so that you can prevent it in the future. Sometimes the cause of and solutions to mistakes are obvious, but when they aren't, a good professional will investigate to figure out what went wrong to make sure that it doesn't happen again.

Correcting mistakes is frequently easier said than done, depending on how bad the error is. Do what you can to make those you've wronged whole with refunds, replacements, or ritual suicide. Doctors whose errors leave patients maimed or dead, engineers whose design miscalculations injure customers, or terrible musicians whose songs steal unrecoverable hours of life from audience members have a hard time making amends. For example, you can never un-hear Soulja Boy's "Crank That" . . .

Apologies are an important part of pull-through after errors. According to Dr. Daryl Koehn of DePaul University, good business apologies have logic, character, and emotion. The lack of any one of these leaves the apology flat and ineffective. Logic means that you understand and can explain what went wrong. Saying "I'm sorry you feel that way" doesn't address the source of the error and won't mean much to someone who believes you've wronged them. The character of the apology includes how timely you are trying to make amends as well as the way in which you plan to make it right with compensation, corrections, or some self-discipline. Expressions of regret don't mean much if they come late or don't include an explanation of the practical steps you'll take to fix the problem. Finally, there is the emotion of the apology. People want a sincere apology, and that means doing it in person, showing empathy for the audience, and following through with changes.

Making amends for mistakes is humbling, and rappers aren't known for their humility. Sean "Diddy" Combs is positively allergic to the whole concept. He crossed a professional line by publicly comparing rival vodkas to urine in an effort to promote his own Ciroc brand. Diddy knew what he'd done wrong. Correcting the situation was as simple as issuing an apology, but what he said didn't make things better. As far as textbook apologies go, it was awful. "I am sorry I came out with these flavors that taste so good . . . I am sorry that the competition's sales are down and we are up. There's nothing I can do about that. I am sorry that I am coming to you live from my bubble bath. I'm not really sorry. It tastes good."[17] But who cares? Sometimes being funny is more valuable than being sorry!

Lose My Mind: Managing Stress and Emotions

The hectic nature of a job is sure to generate stress and amp up emotions. Although the right level of stress can be motivating, and a good leader can use emotions to great effect, knowing how to manage these factors can keep you from losing your mind. We are all emotional beings, and that fact has been helpful to our survival and evolution. Emotions play an important role in life, and it is no surprise that we take them with us to work. However, more often than not, stress and emotions (positive and negative) cloud judgment and obscure facts that can throw off a good business plan. Anger and fear can lead a person to rash or hostile acts. Desire and longing have tripped up more than a few people in the office. Even happiness can interfere with good sense.

It is not necessary to have some scorched-earth policy towards stress and emotions, but recognizing the challenge that they pose is an important part of good health and decision-making. Knowing yourself and the people who work around you is one way to start to identify your triggers: The manager's kid has cancer. The accountant hates country music. The staff in IT can't stand the way the boss talks to them. Emotional triggers can be obvious, or they can be rare and lurking just out of sight. These things affect the work environment. So how do you deal with them?

Many, if not most, decisions at work can stand to wait a bit, so try to slow things down if you or someone else is fired up. Give yourself space and time to think. Physical separation from the source of emotional spurs makes a difference. For example, there is good science to indicate that sleeping on a decision can help a person make a better choice, due in no small part to the steadying effect sleep has on emotional and cognitive activity. If sack time is not an option, sometimes it is enough to just take a few minutes to breathe and focus before moving forward. If that isn't in the cards either, recognize that you are amped up and do the best you can when you pull the trigger . . . well, hopefully, not *literally.*

Who knows? Maybe Kim "Break the Internet" Kardashian married Kanye West because of how deeply in touch with his feelings he was. The Chicago native, rapper, and producer is famous for his eight studio albums, enduring love affair with fashion, contempt for books, and his entertaining inability to control his emotions. Where some of the old-school rappers were cold as ice never letting anyone see them sweat, Kanye wasn't afraid to let it all hang out whether it was a good idea or not. He couldn't let it go when Nike declined to give him a design deal, and Kanye's response was to complain to his fans on stages for months afterwards. Even when million-dollar deals weren't at stake, Kanye could still pitch a fit. "When Jay-Z elected to skip his wedding earlier . . . [in 2014], Kanye West responded by omitting the rapper's name from lyrics during performances."[18]

Whining about Nike didn't increase the global apparel giant's desire to cut Kanye a sweet deal, and his later public failure to check his feelings were unlikely to make Jay-Z want to mend fences. In the business world, most professionals find that kind of drama downright embarrassing. It probably isn't the main reason why his fans follow him, and it definitely wasn't why Roc-A-Fella Records first signed him. So how, exactly, are Kanye's tantrums helping him? Well, if they make Kim Kardashian happy, who are we to criticize?

LIKE A BOSS: HIRING, FIRING, AND HUMAN RESOURCES

FOR THE YEARS THAT THE Rap group N.W.A. was together, they were a Hip-Hop quakenado. The main artists, Eazy-E, DJ Yella, Arabian Prince, Dr. Dre, and Ice Cube, contributed their talents to create two multi-platinum albums. They helped launch a $10 million per month record label, and seized the spotlight in late '80s pop culture. N.W.A. blew up the social status quo with "Fuck tha Police," and they influenced the direction of Hip-Hop for decades. If the band was a business, the artists could hardly have expected to make a bigger splash in the market. They had pegged the needles on every key performance indicators for musicians: money, fame, awards, and fan adoration. It seemed that nothing could stand in their way. Nothing but themselves.

Having achieved significant commercial success, N.W.A. took the relationships that high-performing organizations need to succeed, and they let them go sideways. There was the poor hiring choice of band manager Jerry Heller, whose scheming poisoned the band's collaborative dynamic. There were the financial shenanigans and needless power plays primarily benefiting Eazy-E that compounded the problems, and then there was the horribly mismanaged, mic-dropping departures of Ice Cube and Dr. Dre. Blunders in human resource ultimately killed N.W.A. and generated needless bad blood for years among the Hip-Hop pioneers. Their mistakes were not unique to their organization, nor were they inevitable with the right finesse in personnel management.

Building the 2Live Crew: Hiring

There are few resources as essential to the success of a business as its people. Admittedly, there are solid one-person operations in the economy, but most places couldn't keep the lights on without some additional help for the boss. It doesn't matter how slick the product is, how efficient the machines are, or how well the software runs if the employees are bad. Finding and hiring good employees is one of the most important and underappreciated jobs a manager has. The process has three basic parts: creating the candidate profile, screening applicant resumes, and the interview process.

Hiring starts with knowing the kind of employee the company needs. It can be as simple as setting a salary or wage budget, listing the education required, or describing the work to be done, like graphic design for advertising, installation of custom automation, or providing controlled substances to get faded. That generally leads to job titles that are helpful for creating a job posting. To follow our examples, they would be a graphic designer, industrial engineer, and "street pharmacist." Managers can either create their own job descriptions for the position they need to fill or go online to human resources websites like Monster.com or shrm.org to snag free samples. All of this together provides a candidate profile; this should be posted online, placed in a newspaper if you want to go old school, or take the show on the road to a job fair to attract applicants.

As the resumes roll in, managers should look for candidates with training and experience that matches those identified in the candidate profile. Depending on how many people apply for the position, there are ways to thin the herd. Spotty work history, missing credentials or certifications, gross spelling and grammatical errors, little or no prior experience, and writing the resume in crayon are good discriminators, since they indicate that a person may not have the discipline or experience to serve the company well. Where necessary, companies can commission background checks. Once a manager has an acceptable resume, she can move on to the interview phase.

Maybe saying that Honolulu was an adult male playground is going too far, but it was always a party town. Since at least as far back as World War II, the tourists and the sizable military presence on the island ensured that there were always men looking to get it on. It pretty much guaranteed there would be a thriving sex trade in Hawaii's largest city, and wherever there were prostitutes, there were "sex trade administrators," a position with a very particular set of job skills. While serving on Oahu in the Army, Ice-T would find out if he had what it took to succeed as a pimp.

Mac, a pimp Ice-T met at off-base parties, sized him up as a potential hire in a manner similar to the ways in which modern hiring officials might check out a candidate's Facebook page to see the "real" person. "Mac liked the fact that I could quote Iceberg [Slim, the famous pimp-turned-author], and he started studying me at those parties. I was different from the other infantry dudes since I never drank or smoked . . . 'Dig, you cut out for this here. You cut out for this pimpin' game . . . You don't seem to care about these girls.'"[1] Maybe those qualities wouldn't get Ice-T a job at an insurance company, but he met Mac's candidate profile and screening criteria when a lot of others didn't. Ice-T would be a successful pimp for quite a while.

Similar to the way that Hip-Hop artists make friends and form groups or record labels assess artists for talent and marketability, people in business need to be able to gauge individuals for their suitability in employment. The interview is a quick way to check if a job applicant fits the bill. Initial phone interviews are a good way to narrow the options even further, and a manager can do one in as little as five or ten minutes. You can always get interview questions online, but asking candidates about their work history, reasons for leaving jobs, and describing their best and worst bosses is usually enough for an interviewer to decide whether or not to proceed to a face-to-face interview. Interviewers should trust their instincts. If responses don't make you feel good about a candidate, that is a red flag, and you should move on.

Interviewing and hiring skills require a lot of time and effort to develop and improve, which is why it is vital to practice. One technique to speed up the learning curve is to conduct low-pressure interviews. These are interviews with job seekers who might not be perfect matches for the company because of resume deficiencies, skills gaps, or some other legitimate disqualifying item. Job seekers in these practice sessions can raise interesting questions or highlight company requirements that the hiring agent may not have considered. Low-pressure interviews allow inexperienced recruiters to ask questions and make mistakes, so that when the agent conducts interviews with high-priority job candidates, the process is smoother. Additionally, to be fair to the applicants, people will surprise you with a great interview and career potential.

Group interviews are one way to provide greater scrutiny of a job candidate. Having multiple managers interview the same person at the same time may bring up different discussion topics or aspects of the interviewee in the course of the discussion. Additionally, the company team can compare notes and share different perspectives on the suitability of a potential employee. Repeat interviews of the same candidate are another method to confirm or alter opinions on the viability of someone looking for employment. Be careful to avoid questions about a candidate's age, sex, race, national origin, sexual orientation, family status or composition, religion, or other protected class of information. No job applicant is worth getting sued over because of sloppy interviewing.

It seemed like Mobb Deep switched managers whenever the humidity changed. Their second of many managers was "this dude named Dave" who, it appears, Mobb Deep hired in 1992 because he was "a well-dressed, soft-spoken guy from Queens," with what Albert "Prodigy" Johnson vaguely describes as "a good business mentality." Apparently, this hiring decision was even supported by a third-party psychic . . .[2] We can appreciate Dave's first two qualities since appearance and eloquence can go a long way to make a good first impression. However, there are a couple points worth critiquing. One would hope for a little more definition and detail to a hiring endorsement than "good business mentality." This is where job experience and resume metrics help to support a decision to hire. One might look to see how many groups Dave had managed previously to gauge his experience. How many record labels did he have dealings with? How many contracts had he negotiated? How much money had he secured for his clients during contract negotiations? What additional rights had he secured for artists such as control of master tapes, merchandising, and concert tour earnings? What were his management fees? If he was no longer representing a particular artist, why had the relationship ended?

Initially Prodigy said that Bonz Malone, one of 4th & Broadway's A&R representatives, offered Mobb Deep a $20,000 advance for the album that would be known as *Juvenile Hell*. However, Dave appeared on the scene, and although Prodigy said that he negotiated a good deal, Havoc and Prodigy would walk out with an advance 40 percent smaller than initially offered and a record that sold barely 20,000 copies, causing Mobb Deep to be promptly dropped from the label—not a ringing endorsement for Dave's management skills. Not surprisingly, Havoc and Prodigy fired Dave, but one has to wonder why their psychic didn't see the whole thing coming and warn the rookie artists about the dangers and costs of poor hiring practices.

Asking a psychic for guidance in hiring is certainly unconventional, and we might question Mobb Deep's wisdom on the subject. However, using an outside service to vet job candidates is a popular method for reducing some of the guesswork inherent in the hiring process. Many companies provide a wide range of services to learn more about a potential employee, including intelligence, skills, aptitude, and personality testing. They can verify education and licenses as well as credit and background checks. Testing and investigative organizations can shed light on aspects of a job candidate that may not come out in the course of a routine resume review, phone conversation, or even a face-to-face interview. The tests can help quantify how well a candidate reacts to stress, indicate some of his or her likes and dislikes, and, in some cases, their honesty and integrity. Employers should be careful when using these services. Some state and federal laws place restrictions on an employer's ability to use certain findings or personal history as justification not to hire. The laws are intended to prevent an individual's past mistakes such as criminal convictions, ongoing civil litigation, workers' compensation utilization, poor credit ratings, or bankruptcy from remaining a permanent impediment to finding work.

I'm on a Boat! Onboarding Personnel

Finding and hiring a job candidate is a time-consuming and expensive process. Good onboarding plans for new hires dramatically improve job satisfaction, increase productivity, and help reduce employee turnover, so that companies don't have to repeat the employment process any more than is absolutely necessary. It is a process to get the new employee comfortable and trained in the workplace so that they can provide value to the organization. By asking the question "What would a new hire want to know?" a boss can create a common-sense program to orient someone in the organization. Lists will vary, but some of the baseline items for onboarding include introductions and welcome, company overview, training plan, and supervisor follow-up.

Human beings naturally tend to distrust strangers. It was a survival technique for the unforgiving world of our early species, but it is counterproductive for a company that just spent days, weeks, or months finding someone to integrate with the organization. The modern workplace has little in common with predator-filled savannahs, dark forests, or the gladiator floor of the Roman Coliseum. Well, actually, some places people work are *exactly* like gladiator shows at the Coliseum . . .

Introductions and a welcoming atmosphere help to lower the evolutionary fear of strangers. Direct supervisors should personally take new hires to meet coworkers and learn the workplace layout. The better connected new hires are with their colleagues, the easier it will be training and incorporating the new person to do the job. Managers get bonus points if they can actually remember names and appropriate personal details of both the new guy and the existing staff. If you are one of those people who have the embarrassing inability to remember employees' names, you might want to work on that, because although your team will probably bond after the awkward introductions, it might be at your expense.

When Cordozar Calvin "Snoop Dogg" Broadus started rapping with friends, he knew that if the crew he was forming was going to go far, they would need new talent to balance out some weaknesses. Snoop felt that his good friend Warren "Warren G" Griffin lacked confidence as a rapper, which was a serious liability in the rough-and-tumble Hip-Hop game on the West Coast. Snoop had another friend, Nathaniel Dwayne "Nate Dogg" Hale, who could belt out a tune, and that talent struck Snoop as a skill the group needed. However, just because Snoop wanted Nate Dogg in the group didn't mean that it was a done deal. Warren G was not happy about the new hire. "The reason was simple: G was selfish when it came to our friendship."[3]

Snoop couldn't afford to have G's animosity ruin an important improvement for the group. They were not going to be able to get off the streets of Long Beach without more brass in their sound. Snoop worked to connect G and Nate Dogg.

> *I tried to tell him [Warren G] that there wasn't anybody who could take his place and that Nate was just another brother from the 'hood with some skills who could help us out . . . It wasn't until I got everyone together and we tried out a few things that G cooled off a little and agreed to let Nate be part of the game.*[4]

Snoop knew his people well enough to respond to Warren G's concerns. He worked through awkward welcomes because Snoop knew there was more at stake than just ruffled feathers. "It was cool with me. As far as I was concerned, what mattered most was doing music. And on that count, we were definitely making progress."[5]

Starting at a new job usually involves a mind-numbing stack of paperwork from Human Resources covering a blur of subjects from health insurance selection to direct deposit payroll processing and from home address registration to computer-user setup. Although these details can be irritating, they are essential to the smooth handling of pay, benefits, and regular administration.

Managers should spend some time preparing for this part of an employee's arrival. That means having ready

1. Corporate overview information
2. Pay, tax, health insurance paperwork
3. Workstation/computer setup and logon
4. Security procedures, keys, fobs, time cards, etc.
5. Workplace safety training

The better and easier the in-processing goes, the higher opinion the new employee will have of the organization.

Even in Hip-Hop, when you look past the honey-stacked entourages, snow-blinding bling, scandalous VIP-room adventures, and globetrotting concert tours, there is the unsexy business of paperwork and corporate overviews. For Hip-Hop stars, that starts with the record contracts and terms of employment with the label, managers, and lawyers. History has lots of examples of poor administration, and it has led to the downfall of more than a few record labels. In their time, Sugar Hill Records, Profile Records, and Death Row Records were major fixtures of the Hip-Hop world. Unfortunately, they all mismanaged artists' basic interests like bonuses, royalties, and other benefits—and not just on a handful of occasions. The fallout from those failures ultimately did in the labels, so getting the administrative part of onboarding right is as good for the company as it is for the employee.

Even when a company finds a plug-and-play employee, there is usually still some kind of job familiarization necessary to get the new person up and running. Creating a training plan gives managers the opportunity to ensure that a new hire gets exposure to all the things they need on the job. It gives the employee a sense of structure and focus during the critical first steps in the position, and the more effective the training, the quicker the company and new team member start benefiting.

Hip-Hop did not enjoy a warm embrace from most radio stations for a long time after it arrived on the scene, but eventually some started to come around to the new sound and the culture it represented. Los Angeles' Power 106 decided that it would be the home of Hip-Hop in SoCal. But the decision to be a youth-oriented, Hip-Hop-playing radio station did not guarantee success. The station struggled with broadcasting an authentic voice and focusing on the listeners and their needs. It wasn't enough just to play a song that kids liked. Anyone could do that. Power 106's staff needed training to connect better with its customer base.

Rick Cummings, who had launched the station in 1986, recognized that his staff did not perfectly reflect the demographics of the listeners and the world in which they lived, so he created a plan to make the station more responsive. He brought in Manny Velazquez, a local crisis-intervention worker, whose experience and reputation working with gangs and violence in the community gave him immediate street cred.

Velazquez returned and gave the staff a three-hour seminar on gang life in Los Angeles. He ended the session by offering to take them on a cruise of the neighborhoods in which he worked.[6]

The lessons were timely and effective. When the Rodney King Riots of 1992 engulfed South Central Los Angeles following the acquittal "of the police officers who beat Rodney King, Power 106 debuted their new public affairs show, 'From the Streets,' hosted by Frank Lozano and Manny Velazquez."[7] The training and staff change made Power 106 the go-to station for angry young people who needed a voice. Even after the violence abated, the station had earned enduring loyalty from its listeners and the economic benefits that went with it. Not too shabby for on-the-job training.

In order to be sure that things stay on track with new hires, supervisors have got to follow up with them. There are lots of chances for things to go off the rails even when introductions, administration, and training are all done right. The best way for a manager to stay ahead of problems with new employees is by checking in regularly. Follow-up gives the newbie a time when they can bring up issues, and it is an opportunity for the supervisor to make changes to keep things straight. The contacts help build rapport and improve productivity and job satisfaction.

When Sean "P Diddy" Combs left Uptown Records to start his own label, he had a need to succeed; so, for his marquee talent, Diddy signed the strongest sound in East Coast Rap, The Notorious B.I.G., Christopher George Latore Wallace. Biggie had a "candid Rapping style, which, operating much in the spirit of the drug trade he had come up in, took no shorts."[8] But even though he was an incredible lyricist and rapper, Diddy wouldn't simply trust the talent of his new star to make his fortune. Biggie was good, but Diddy wanted to make sure that when his debut album came out, it would be positively historic.

As executive producer for *Ready to Die*, Diddy spent nearly two years working directly with Biggie.[9] The two of them had their own ideas about how Biggie's music should sound, but their close collaboration allowed them to work through their differences. Together they learned to correct the timing, tweak the sounds, and polish the tracks that would earn the album a double platinum certification, with more than two million copies sold. Biggie might have been a hit anywhere, but Diddy's follow-up and engagement with him guaranteed that The Notorious B.I.G. would be a legend.

Variety Is the Spice 1 of Life: Workplace Diversity

Studies consistently show that diversity strengthens organizations. It works somewhat like physical exercise. It might not always feel good in the hard times, but, when done properly, the results are almost always positive. While there are good political and ethical reasons for promoting diversity, it creates opportunities for growth and challenges conventional wisdom, which can prevent the complacency and group-think that kill companies.

Business leaders need to know how to manage diversity, whether a company is a rural machine shop or colossal multinational corporation. That is because the same benefits of success (like sales growth, customer and employee loyalty, and innovation) and dangers of failure (such as boycotts, lawsuits, and lost sales) exist for all of them. Diversity is not about following quota sets in hiring. Instead, it is about organizational adaptability to create the environment where qualified candidates can play their part. To that end, leadership has to encourage a marketplace of ideas, hire with an open mind, and prepare to work through conflict.

The marketplace of ideas is the most important piece of diversity. If a company cannot sustain this foundational concept, the rest is unlikely to follow. Teams can create the marketplace any time a decision needs to be made using different opinions and perspectives. Even minor distinctions among people, backgrounds, and jobs can be helpful when trying to generate fresh thinking; but the wider the variations, the more interesting the ideas are likely to be during problem solving. Pilots might have similar baseline training to one another, but if they fly different types of aircraft, they are likely to view the world from unique perspectives. Similarly, pilots and financial analysts are likely to have widely different assessments of a situation when provided the same data. The skills, abilities, and outlook diverse people bring can offer solutions to problems that like-minded, homogenous groups might never consider. That is a big part of the diversity a company needs to seek.

When Wu-Tang front man Robert Fitzgerald "RZA" Diggs came up with a plan to take the Hip-Hop market by storm, diversity was critical to the Clan's success. However, by the standards of the federal and state Equal Employment Opportunity offices responsible for combatting harassment of and discrimination toward protected classes of people, one might not have considered the Wu-Tang Clan very diverse. The Wu-Tang Clan and even its associated bands were almost exclusively African-American. So what was the diversity RZA wanted so badly? His plan called for a mixture of ideas and musical styles to capture market share in Hip-Hop.

At the time, the Hip-Hop music market was about one-third the size of the Rock music market in sales terms.[10] According to RZA's calculations, that meant it was small enough to blanket with Wu-Tang-associated artists.

> *The ultimate aim of my long-term plan was to take over one-third of the industry. I counted how many Hip-Hop artists there were and how many artists I had, and I realized that we could do it.*[11]

The Wu-Tang Clan would need artists stylistically and musically different from one another who could fill the various niches in Hip-Hop's sound and culture. For fans of the music, each artist and affiliate band was different. For example, there was Dennis "Ghostface Killah" Coles who was loud, fast, and used his own slang inventions. Corey Quontrell "Raekwon" Woods helped pioneer Mafioso Rap, which was an effective competitor to West Coast Gangsta Rap. An affiliate Wu-Tang Clan band, Sunz of Man, filled their songs with social issues and biblical stories.

Within the spectrum of mid-1990s Hip-Hop, the Wu-Tang Clan had cultivated a mixture that could reach the wide-ranging fan base in a big way. As RZA watched Wu-Tang artists and affiliates spread from record label to record label releasing gold, platinum, and multi-platinum albums, he was ecstatic with the results of his diversity program's success.

The marketplace of ideas is key to diversity, but open-minded hiring is where a company's multicultural features become more real. Recognizing the value that different people bring to work is not always easy or comfortable. Business leaders have to stress the economic advantages of diverse employees for the organization and balance them with the skills and abilities of actual job candidates. A corporation that is unable to accommodate the give-and-take that comes with some diversity on the staff will probably have trouble helping customers—who are rarely a monolithic group—solve their problems. Remember that solving customer problems is how a business makes money. However, managers should never hire unqualified applicants for a job just to "add diversity."

The Hip-Hop community was rightfully proud of its majority Black artist roster. They were responsible for Hip-Hop culture and music being home to free expression on race, justice, economics, and politics. Those topics regularly combined in hit songs and albums that fans felt deeply. None of this is to say that Hip-Hop was exclusionary. Vanilla Ice and the Beastie Boys had long ago proven that Whites could succeed as rappers. That is, if we can say that Vanilla Ice was successful . . . Still, Hip-Hop's most famous diversity hire had to be Eminem. The skinny White kid from Detroit was controversial for a lot of reasons, but his skin color was an issue to a lot of people when Dr. Dre decided to bring him to Aftermath Entertainment.

Dre knew he was gambling with his hard-earned reputation signing the unknown artist, but Dre also knew two other things that were essential to his decision. First, after hearing him audition, Dre knew that Eminem was an extremely good rapper, so he was qualified. Second, according to commercial data from a variety of sources, most Hip-Hop fans were White. "A White kid would be a change of pace, and Dre, who was married to a White woman, felt a Caucasian could say things he couldn't."[12] That was part of the value for Aftermath. "And the mere fact that he, Dr. Dre, was working with him would give Em credibility."[13] That mentorship was priceless.

Dr. Dre hired and supported Eminem for all the right reasons. He was a highly qualified, street-tested rapper. He added a new and valuable voice to the Hip-Hop scene. Oh, and he made a metric shit-ton of money for Aftermath Entertainment by being the highest selling artist in Hip-Hop. That was probably worth noting, too . . .

Anyone who's ever seen identical twin siblings fight knows that similarity is no guarantee of peace; so, naturally, whenever conflict-prone animals like human beings have even mild differences thrown into the mix, trouble may be right around the corner. It just isn't reasonable to expect anything else. As a result, managers must prepare to work through conflicts as part of a diverse environment. Good conflict management allows people to be people with their inevitable beefs, but it keeps the workplace violence to less-than-lethal levels. However, don't think referee service is absolutely essential. Bosses could always trust luck, reasonable physical fitness, and good shoes to safely make the dash from the office to the getaway car before the torch-wielding mob of angry workers comes for them.

There are volumes written on conflict management. The best lessons on the subject come down to open communication, honest brokers, and the will to enforce rules. Whether people are "fronting over some trifling BS" or harmed by a serious offense, open and honest communication is the only thing that is going to expose the truth. Supervisors need to find the sources of conflict by asking questions to allow people to tell their story. Managers with near-magical powers can use their skills to actually prevent conflicts before they happen just by engaging their people and checking on tensions before they flare up.

The honest-broker piece of conflict management is about being a neutral intermediary that the rival factions can trust.

Without the trust of the people battling it out, any ruling from authority figures will have no credibility with the parties. It raises the likelihood that the conflict will persist and that someone is going to scrawl "No Justice, No Peace" all over the breakroom walls. Business leaders can build up their honest-broker cred by avoiding favoritism, nepotism, and general douchebagery at work. Bosses who find basic human decency too difficult should seek out someone who *does* meet the requirements to get the drama under control.

The final step in conflict management is rule enforcement. After getting good feedback from the workplace gladiators by putting on their most sincere facial expressions, managers have to do *something* about the problems they've investigated. Wise leaders will use a mixture of good judgment, company policy, and the authority that comes only from channeling a gaudy reality-TV show host to tell the staff how it's going to be. After that, it is up to the manager to follow through. If an employee cannot abide by the law after you lay it down, well, sometimes heads have got to roll.

There are plenty of times in Hip-Hop when conflict was addressed in a sober, mature, and adult fashion, when each side saw the truth in the other's viewpoint and parted ways with kind words and greater mutual respect. But you didn't buy this book for that crap. Let's give you something juicy.

Earl "DMX" Simmons had a lot of strikes against him from robbing simple cabbies who couldn't afford to lose the $50–$60 he jacked,[14] to selling his own fans blank tapes he claimed had his music,[15] to the generally disreputable abuse of animals he seemed to enjoy so much with his pit bull. DMX did enough stupid shit that even ethically challenged Suge Knight decided to keep his distance from the Rap star.[16] Sure, X had a few good tunes to his name. He even made some decent money for a while. But the dick moves he pulled again and again in his own neighborhood ensured that he would never be able to count on anyone to back him up when things got real.

One night in Yonkers, New York, DMX found himself walking around followed by the mile-long train of relationship baggage he'd created for himself from years of idiocy. It happened that, at the same time, a large group of guys was looking to settle a score for some local robberies that, for once, X wasn't responsible for. When they found X, the excrement made contact with the oscillating air-distribution device. Words got heated, and the situation escalated fast.

Perhaps among the unidentified assembly there was someone who could have tried an open dialogue with those gathered. Maybe he could have been an honest broker that both sides could have trusted to adjudicate the matter. Perchance he could even have enforced law and order over the two sides. If that guy was on the street that night, he took one look at DMX and said, "Fuck it." The result was that Earl "DMX" Simmons got the epic, multiparty, 55-gallon drum of Alabama ass whooping that he had desperately being crying for. Payback for him was a real bitch.

> . . . *it was obvious that most of my family had written me off. I knew that they heard what happened and how bad it was—the story of DMX getting beaten up was all over Yonkers by that next afternoon—but that didn't seem to motivate any of them to knock on the door or even pick up the phone.*[17]

You reap what you sow, X, so take that. The rest of the world, on the other hand, should take good conflict management seriously.

W.E.R.K.: Development and Delegation

Business leaders have all kinds of important obligations: meeting ambitious corporate profit targets, controlling rising departmental expenses, grappling with aggressive marketplace competition, and carefully crafting cover stories to obstruct federal regulators. Yes, some people have a lot to pack in to the workday from its grueling kickoff at a mid-morning champagne brunch to its exhausting end with an early-afternoon golf scramble. No matter how good managers are, they can't and shouldn't do everything alone. Effectively delegating work to others is crucial to growth because it frees leaders to do other things, maximizes worker productivity, and provides opportunity for development and growth for everyone involved. Good task assignments demand that supervisors communicate and train their people to be able to do the work and provide the right oversight so the job is done well.

In keeping with the recurring theme, managers have to know what needs to get done so that they can describe "what done looks like" to the workers who will ultimately have to do the work. Understanding the job gives the boss the ability to decide if it's is a good idea to delegate it. There are duties vital for a company's long-term success over which managers should maintain control, like financing, major contract approval, and the hiring of key personnel. Some jobs have tight deadlines and complex tasks that make passing off the work to someone else impractical. Delegation works best in other responsibilities like recurring and routine tasks like machine maintenance or product distribution. It is good for worker-growth opportunities like project management, capacity-expanding prospects like logistic-solution studies, or software research and development.

Once a boss picks out the jobs to delegate, the next step is picking a team member to do the work. There are basically two kinds of workers: "plug-and-play" types and "projects." Plug-and-play employees probably already know most of the basics of the work required and need only a little instruction on the what, how, when, and why of a job. These human easy buttons make life in leadership pretty sweet since they don't need much babysitting. Wind them up, and watch them go. It's awesome. The other type of worker, "projects," require time and patience from supervisors. Their inexperience makes it necessary to explain tasks, review instructions and procedures, and double-check the finished product for quality assurance. All of that takes effort, but the benefits of getting team members experience with a variety of work usually outweigh the costs of the time it takes to hand off a job properly.

Supervisors who delegate the execution of tasks don't delegate the ultimate responsibility for how well the work gets done. Bosses are accountable for the end results, so to avoid surprises and embarrassment, they have to follow up. There is a fine line between simple quality checks on a subordinate's work and micromanagement. Bosses should know what are essential deliverables. If a team member provides the essentials but does it in an unexpected way, that should not be a problem. Basically, don't sweat the small stuff. Managers can save themselves and their subordinates a lot of anxiety by discussing expectations for how often they will check in and setting deadlines for work.

Indie artists Ben "Macklemore" Haggerty and Ryan Lewis might not have created the intersection of hipster and Hip-Hop culture, but they certainly exploited it. Their hits "Same Love," "Thrift Shop," and "Can't Hold Us," from *The Heist,* peaked at number one on the *Billboard* Hot 100, with each scoring millions of downloads. The Hip-Hop duo had full schedules with studio time, interviews, public appearances, and performances on tour. There were not enough hours in the day to do all of things necessary to make that possible by themselves. Honestly, Macklemore and Lewis didn't have the expertise to handle all the music management. The two artists wisely recognized that they needed help as stars. That is where Zach Quillen entered the picture.

Operating without being signed to a major label that would back the group, Macklemore and Lewis needed the expertise that Quillen brought. As the group's manager, Quillen was able to relieve Macklemore and Lewis of administrative tasks that freed them up to play the public roles of Hip-Hop stars. The two artists' direction to Quillen was simple: make us big. That was totally doable with his background in the business. The new manager was a plug-and-play hire because he had previously booked tours for Wiz Khalifa and the lesser-known Blue Scholars. That meant that Macklemore and Lewis didn't need to spend time explaining in detail what they wanted done. Quillen could take over marketing roles that he was well suited to manage. He led efforts to engage fans on a slew of social media platforms to build buzz. The artists checked his work as measured by sold-out show after sold-out show. The hype that Quillen created behind the scenes following Macklemore's and Lewis's direction had a lot to do with *The Heist* winning the Grammy in the Hip-Hop category. That is good delegation right there.

Personnel Assesstimates: Staff Evaluations

Charles Darwin, the English naturalist and big daddy of evo-lutionary science, described life in the natural world in constant competition. The workplace is not radically different, and bosses need to be able to judge their workers for how well they meet company needs to survive the market competition. In a world of complexity, evaluations can be remarkably easy. There are essentially only two things to look at: a worker's skills and atti-tude. Staff members should have a good idea of what constitutes solid-gold or epic-fail performance after spending countless hours creating departmental goals, searching for qualified job candi-dates, and debating the meat and potatoes of the job. Evaluations are useful because the modern workforce wants to know how it is doing. Team members whose work benefits the company and who help it to adapt have to be recognized, rewarded, and retained. Those who don't meet standards need to be helped to improve or need to see that they would be happier elsewhere. Job performance reviews are a great format to accomplish that.

The evaluation process should be a mix of formal and informal feedback given regularly and based on well-understood job goals and expectations. Informally, supervisors should check in with their people directly, asking them how work is going and providing comments on progress. These can be as straightforward as talking in the hallway or workstation. Meetings like these are the best chance for managers to help employees to make little improvements and prevent small problems from going nuclear. They are also useful as the basis to create a paper trail when things aren't going well and they are on their way to termination. If bosses do their job by setting and communicating expectations, then the difficult chore of correcting employees is a little bit easier. Still not fun, but easier . . .

Formal feedback can take the form of the dreaded semiannual or annual written evaluation. Although the system has fallen out of favor at many organizations, formal reviews can serve as the backstop for frontline supervisors. Bosses are pulled in a million directions every day, and the informal feedback sessions just discussed are frequently the first casualties of a busy manager's overbooked schedule. Who has time to chitchat about the small stuff? Companies that require formal reviews will ensure that, at least once a year, a supervisor is going to have to discuss job performance with an employee. The once-a-year formal feedback should be the bare minimum because it is definitely not the gold standard for personnel evaluations.

Whether an employee is knocking the ball out of the park or can barely fog a mirror during work, managers need to be honest in their assessments. Bad news doesn't get better with age, so just tell employees when there is a problem. People can fix only the things they know about. Managers who lack the intestinal fortitude to give a less-than-glowing review can always resort to the suggestions available on *passiveaggressivenotes.com* or *genuineevaluation.com*. They provide a range of feedback options from starched-shirt, professional power phrases to biting sarcasm to express displeasure. Constructive criticism should come with some kind of employee assistance. Organizations that have the resources and time should offer all existing employees a pathway to promotion with appropriate training opportunities and enough encouragement to keep them motivated. This increases the likelihood of a fairer and more equitable assessment and promotion system.

As far as drug dealers go, 50 Cent was a pretty good one. 50 had a winning attitude that kept him out on the street hustling long past the time when less-dedicated candymen and pushers would shuffle home. He had the skills to manufacture and package his own product in a way that guaranteed him a higher profit margin. He knew how to bring in sales from regulars and new customers alike. 50 was even good at protecting himself and keeping the police at bay. Drug dealers frequently enjoy a looser connection with their bosses than, say, medical interns have from their attending physicians while doing rounds in an intensive care unit. Even so, there was a little bit of a supervisor-subordinate relationship between drug suppliers, gang leaders, and their dealers, in which employee evaluations had a place, and 50 Cent benefited from that supervisor coaching and evaluation.

One of 50's superiors, a guy named Brian, critiqued him on how he blew through money without saving up a reserve. Brian instructed 50 on how to properly mix cocaine and common household chemicals to create crack. The regional drug distributor for Queens, some dude named Carlos, reviewed 50's performance compared to some other lower-quality dealers. Carlos explained that 50 was doing his job well. He paid his supplier debts on time, sold his product regularly, satisfying his customer base, and he projected strength without attracting the wrong kind of attention from rival gangs or cops. In fact, based on the positive reviews, Carlos promoted 50 from retail dealers selling small ounce quantities to wholesale dealers, a more prestigious and easier sales position.

Brian and Carlos knew what they expected from dealers, and they were able to communicate those expectations to 50 Cent. They gave him regular feedback to improve his performance, and they didn't pull punches when they thought 50 was screwing up. If there were more regular working hours, employer-provided health insurance, and the paperwork from 50's annual evaluation properly filed with HR, the whole bunch of them could have been working in a different part of the drug industry for giants like AstraZeneca, GlaxoSmithKline, Pfizer, or Merck.

Beat Downs: Discipline on the Job

It is an unfortunate reality, but there are times when people go down the wrong path at work. And at times like that, it is the boss' job to regulate with appropriate discipline, up to and including termination. In a culture where we try to be agreeable and avoid causing offense, the idea of taking negative employment action against someone at work can be distasteful. However, discipline is nothing but enforcing standards, and it is a natural and healthy process that actually cares for employees and the organization. Managers who cannot bring themselves to make tough calls doom their companies to mediocrity and worse by allowing bad behavior, poor performance, and generally disreputable conduct. It can kill morale and lower productivity with good employees, proving the rule that one bad apple can spoil the whole barrel.

Supervising behavior and performance is just one small part of the assessment-and-feedback process discussed earlier. The only difference is that, for discipline, the focus is specifically negative. It should be well documented, progressive, consistent, and definitive. When properly done, it can be a relatively clean process that can take a company to a higher level. Botch the job, and a company can look forward to some dark days of disgruntled workers, dissatisfied customers, lost sales, and even legal action.

When a team member just doesn't measure up, supervisors have got to document their discussions with the offender. Verbal warnings are great tools that can help get people back on track, but they don't create the paper trail that supports more serious negative employment actions like demotion and firing. If and when those times arrive, paperwork can save a lot of legal trouble. Documentation doesn't have to be complicated. A couple lines about the incident on an e-mail sent to the employee, HR, or next-higher manager may be enough for record-keeping purposes. Managers who get employees to sign off on the contents of their negative-feedback session score extra points.

Kwame Kilpatrick billed himself as the "Hip-Hop mayor of Detroit." He had previously been a Michigan state representative when, at the age of 31, he became the Motor City's youngest mayor. There was a certain air of enthusiasm around the new leader as he came into office in 2002. He was incredibly smart, well educated, well dressed, had good tastes in music, and he knew how to throw a baller party for supporters. All of that had helped him win the election, beating his closest rival by 50 percent total votes. There was a lot of hope in Detroit that Kilpatrick could turn things around for the troubled hometown of Hip-Hop greats like Proof, J Dilla, Big Sean, and Eminem. If Hip-Hop could help make Kilpatrick mayor, maybe, together, Hip-Hop and Kilpatrick could make Detroit great again. But that wasn't how things went down.

While the city continued to sink into decline and eventual bankruptcy, signs of bribery, fraud, and racketeering at the mayor's office were barely concealed. Local and federal investigators went about meticulously documenting the offenses over years. When the state finally presented its case at Kilpatrick's trial, the overwhelming evidence of abuse of power, corruption, and tax evasion was enough to put the Hip-Hop mayor in the federal corrections institute in Oklahoma with a 28-year sentence. Hopefully, when dealing with problem employees at your workplace you aren't dealing with corruption deep enough to sink a city; but even if you do, document your case, and maybe you'll be able to stop the slide before it's too late.

Discipline at work should generally be progressive. There are offenses for which immediate termination is justified, like workplace violence, gross safety violations, and other ethical failures. Setting those exceptions aside, the purpose of negative feedback is to correct a problem, not eliminate a person. The path of progressive discipline leads from verbal warnings through written documentation and on to termination. Managers should explain what happens the next time there is a repeat violation during the counseling session with a team member.

When he was still a teenager, Snoop worked stocking shelves at a small grocery store called Lucky's on Long Beach Boulevard. Snoop got fired from his job when he got high with his friends, showing up an hour late. His manager kicked him straight out the door. Despite his high, Snoop didn't feel so good later, when he realized that he'd have to tell his mother what had happened. Sure, the manager could have tried to handle things in a stair-step approach with a written warning. But given Snoop's short tenure with the company, his less-than-stellar work performance, and the combination of tardiness and drug use, the incident is a fair example of a legitimate "shooting offense."

Consistency in discipline is an under-appreciated virtue by managers. Workers have another word for consistency: fairness. If a company is going to enforce a rule, it needs to enforce the rule across the board—one rule for everyone. The news is filled with stories of organizations with double standards, workplace harassment, and rampant discrimination. All of these are failures to apply the enforcement standards evenly, and the fact that the companies are in the news is evidence of how failure to stay consistent can cost a company its reputation . . . oh, and a crap-ton of money in settlements.

The Internet changed everything for the music industry. By 2000, the old model for selling music—sign, record, release, wash, rinse, repeat—were dead. Piracy and direct-to-consumer content ate into profit margins so that record labels could not support a large stable of second-tier artists. If you weren't selling above a certain rate, the labels started to cut acts loose. Executives at Universal Music Group reached into subordinate labels and cut staff by 75 percent in some cases. At Aftermath Entertainment, Dr. Dre cleared his entire roster. "Eve, Last Emperor, Dawn Robinson, King Tee, and most artists and producers . . . were out."[18]

The layoffs at Universal and Aftermath were hard on the artists who were cut, but both companies conducted their layoffs with a cold consistency. A band could perform and sell records at a level that could generate profit for the label, or the artists were out. It was cold, and it was unpleasant. But it was clear, and it was consistent. People can understand that . . . even if they don't like it.

Rule enforcement should be definitive. Once a boss takes negative employment action, the ruling has to stand. Supervisors who've documented an employee's failures and enforced rules fairly should feel secure that they are making good decisions. Weak-kneed, mealy-mouthed backsliding on discipline will blow up a manager's reputation and make future efforts to maintain standards more difficult. Why would anyone have faith in corrective actions if they know that a manager is just going to reverse the decision with the right amount of whining, tears, or threats? The world isn't black and white, but if you decide to back off on a disciplinary judgment, you'd better have a very good reason for it that you can explain to a court.

To hear Snoop tell the story, the Insane Crips Gang were some "vicious motherfuckers."

> *The ICG would as soon cut you wide open as look at you and nobody, but nobody, had the balls to fuck with them. They were rabid dogs set loose on the neighborhood, and I still get a cold chill sometimes thinking about them.*[19]

Even though the ICG was loosely allied with Snoop's own Rolling 20 Crips group, he knew better than to screw around with them. The ICG didn't make threats. They made promises. The bodies in the streets were proof enough of that, and that decisiveness made the ICG's job of enforcing control over the neighborhood much, much easier. The fact that Snoop remembered their chilling record so clearly years later when he wrote his book demonstrates the effectiveness of consistency. Legitimate businesspeople would do well to take note of some of the ICG's discipline process. You should probably just go a little bit easier on the murder and mayhem . . .

Dead Man Walking: Terminations and Layoffs

In 1999, Mobb Deep's Prodigy met a group called Bars'N'Hooks, a pair of rappers from the Hip-Hop star's hometown of Queensbridge, New York. P was toying with his own record label, the relatively unknown Infamous Records. He liked what he saw in Bars'N'Hooks. They dressed sharply. They had reputations in the neighborhood, and they could spit verses, particularly dissing Nas, Prodigy's archrival. That was enough to get Bars'N'Hooks in the door at Infamous, but it would not be enough to keep them there.

Prodigy tried to do right by the new artists, promoting two of their singles using a national DJ list and mailing out recordings.

Bars'N'Hooks then proceeded to crater their unborn careers epically. They started by breaking into and robbing Havoc, the second half of Mobb Deep and Prodigy's best friend. They tried to fence their loot on the same neighborhood streets where the evidence of their misdeeds was obvious. They traded in a blue Mercedes Benz P had given them in favor of a black Excursion on which they owed $15,000. Prodigy couldn't believe he'd signed these clowns to his label.

> *"So, you sold the chain and the Benz to get a truck that you can't afford, and you robbed Havoc's crib?" I said. "What's wrong with you, man?" You just fucked everything up for us. I severed my ties with Bars'N'Hooks. How stupid could you be?*[20]

P was never the best businessman in Hip-Hop, but even he had the good sense to recognize when an employment relationship just didn't work.

If coaching and correction fail to bring an employee back onto the path of righteousness, or if market conditions make a reorganization and layoffs necessary, business leaders have the unenviable responsibility of carrying out "involuntary resource actions," another polite euphemism for shit-canning people. People spend a lot of time at work, so ending someone's employment can be an emotional and difficult process. When things go sideways, a boss needs to know how to end the pain quickly, cleanly, and as painlessly as possible. Closing out a team member's tenure at the company the right way allows the whole organization to move on.

The termination process can take an unfortunate situation and make it into something that builds credibility for an organization's leadership. Properly shaping a company through discharges can actually create a stronger company by eliminating problem employees, reducing costs, and adding efficiencies. Firings and layoffs are similar in effect but different in causation and motivation. Some of the essentials of a good breakup are true for both employment-ending categories. Terminations should be justified, planned, direct, quick, and compassionate, and they should create closure. Since layoff events are usually not the employees' fault, they should include all of the previous list and transition assistance and severance when appropriate.

If someone has to go out the door, it should be for good reasons. Incompetence, poor performance, insubordination, mismanagement, toxic attitudes, ethical breaches, and dozens of others are all legitimate reasons to end someone's employment. However, there are lots of bad reasons people get fired, too. Sadly, there are organizations that use pink slips as reprisals against protected acts like labor organizing, whistleblowing, and serious complaints. Other companies have gone after protected-classes people for age, sex, sexual orientation, religion, national origin, race, color, and/or creed. Those are serious violations of labor laws, and in addition to being a dick move, it is a sign of managerial laziness. Seriously, how hard is it to do this right?

Managers should review an employee's disciplinary documentation for firings or prepare layoff justification with Human Resources. The material should be clear enough to speak for itself to an outsider. Once the documentation and explanations are prepared, there are advantages to scripting how the termination will go. Role-playing can be helpful for skittish first-time "terminators." Agreeing on who will be there in the room and practicing what to say to an employee who the company is separating can reduce anxieties and smooth out responses for the real thing. The company should be ready to reclaim its property, such as phones, computers, keys, and to shut down access to systems for any terminated personnel. The management team will also need a strategy for packing up the employee's belongings and escorting them out. Any reasonable event from calling the soon-to-be-ex-employee into an office for "the talk" through to their departure from the property should be discussed. A well-planned employment-ending event keeps the unpleasantness of the whole thing to a minimum.

If someone is going to be in leadership, they have got to have a proverbial "pair." If someone is getting canned, they would like to think their boss has the stones to do it to their face . . . metaphorically speaking . . . Meeting directly is a sign of respect, and most employees have done enough good things during their tenure at work to deserve that. Face-to-face meetings do not mean going it alone. Managers can and should bring in another supervisor or company representative to act as a witness and provide some moral support at a difficult time.

The meeting should be compassionate and quick. Get the employee off the floor and into someplace private. Once the employee is in the office, explain what is happening to them. It is not a discussion. You are not there to argue about facts. This is actually happening, but be polite. There is no professional advantage in terminating someone publicly or getting fired up in the meeting. The cooler the company representatives can play it, the better the chance they have of a clean break with the employee. Botch the job, and the probability of your former coworker lawyering up and coming after the organization goes way up.

Barring litigation, the last step in terminations is to create closure. That means filing termination paperwork, scheduling coverage for the vacant position, and explaining the changes to other members of the staff. In medium- and large-sized companies there is almost always red tape to deal with when wrapping up someone's employment: 401(k) accounts, COBRA insurance, computer or accounting system access, accrued vacation payouts, final paychecks, etc. Small companies have the same issues, but they are just less likely to have personnel and formal processes to address these situations. Communicating to the staff basic details of the termination and the plan to cover schedules, routine tasks, and special responsibilities is critical to a smooth transition following someone's departure. People can be anxious about personnel changes at work, so a good explanation can reduce gossip and get people focused on life without their ex-colleague.

The creative destruction inherent in the capitalist system guarantees that layoffs will always exist. This kind of dismissal should include all of the things we just covered, but good companies add in a couple things for the unfortunate victims of corporate reorganizations: transition assistance and severance when appropriate. Transition assistance for laid-off employees can be letters of recommendation, connecting with employment recruiters, resume writing, or helping qualified workers file for Social Security, Medicare, or disability benefits. The softer a company can make the impact of a layoff for an employee, the better everyone will feel—both those who go out the door and those left at work. Both groups will be glad that the company tried to do right by its people at a tough time. Not every organization will be able to afford it, but severance payments can ease the financial stress of an employee's situation. A conservative figure may be one week of pay for every two years of service, but industry norms and the company's financial constraints may dictate more- or less-generous severance terms. A quick Google search can clear up questions on common practice for similarly sized companies in the market. In fact, transition assistance and severance can even be dangled to employees being fired if it helps make the break cleaner.

Sean "P Diddy" Combs wasn't the easiest guy in the world to work with. While working for Andre Harrell at Uptown Records, Diddy helped the label sell more than 10 million records in six years. The wildly successful sales of its artists attracted the attention of MCA Records, which wanted to turn Uptown sales into

MCA profits. In mid-1992 MCA inked a deal with Uptown that infused $50 million for operations, which required the label to increase its already frantic pace of hit productions.[21] But as so often happens in the case of mergers and acquisitions, there was a culture clash between MCA and Uptown staff. Well, maybe the clash was just between Diddy and MCA . . .

MCA wanted Uptown expenses controlled, and Andre Harrell had to find someone to do what it took to satisfy MCA. Diddy couldn't live with the changes. He was disruptive and hostile to the new MCA-approved team leaders at Uptown. Harrell wasn't happy with the increasing conflict, and he didn't want to have to take negative employment actions because he genuinely liked and respected Diddy. However, as a boss, he recognized that things weren't working out.

Although Harrell didn't involve armies of HR professionals in discussions, he still created a plan that would end Diddy's time with Uptown Records. Once he was ready, Harrell called Combs into his office and told him he was letting him go. The talk was straight to the point, even though Diddy was fuming. To soften the blow, make sure that he didn't create any more hard feelings than were necessary, and out of respect for how talented he thought he was, Harrell offered Diddy a lavish severance package. He kept the young producer on Uptown's payroll almost indefinitely. Diddy would collect checks for months, and that freed him financially and professionally to create Bad Boy Records, the label that would launch Hip-Hop legends like Biggie Smalls, Rick Ross, and The Lox. The clean break allowed both labels to prosper for a while after each party went its own way.

WORKMAGEDDON: PROJECT MANAGEMENT

L OTS OF THINGS GO INTO making a business work, and
every company will have its own practices and routines in
dealing with continuing marketplace challenges. However, one
skill set seems particularly valuable for entrepreneurs who face
well-defined, individual challenges: project management. It is the
application of tools, know-how, and skills to project activities
to get the job done, satisfy the stakeholders, and make a little
money, too.

Tracy "Ice-T" Marrow was, bar none, the best project manager
in the history of Hip-Hop. He brought organization and planning
to everything he did in a way that had never been seen before and
has not been repeated since in the genre. His whole professional
life has been one well-managed project after another. While he
attributes a lot of it to his training in the US Army, something
says that Ice-T was just uniquely suited to bring order into the
chaotic worlds he chose to inhabit.

Ice-T stood up a respectable prostitution ring (relatively speaking) in Hawaii by defining his objectives, figuring the scope of
the operation, and understanding the deliverables he and his

women had to produce. He created one of the most effective smash-and-grab gangs in L.A., which hauled in hundreds of thousands of dollars in loot from dozens of successful individual jobs by creating a set of plans to help guide his team through every step of the job. When Ice-T started to play in the Rap game, he hammered on deliverables that his fans and customers demanded all the while juggling the logistical challenges that went with rounding up supplies and communicating with people who needed to hear his sound.

As his music progressed from its beginning into the big time, Marrow monitored and controlled almost every aspect of his career, making sure that it met with the approval of his various stakeholders: money for his family, revenue and prestige for his record label, and hardcore, bass-pumping entertainment for his fans. Ice-T even had the self-awareness to recognize that no project can last forever, and he achieved one of the most dignified closing processes to any Hip-Hop career as he left the center stage of Hip-Hop and transitioned into other successful roles in television and film entertainment.

Ice-T appreciated that following project-management methods lowered his risks, reduced his costs, and improved his chances of success. If it could work in pimping, high-intensity robbery, Rap, and entertainment, it could work in any industry. All you have to do is understand and apply the process and techniques in the five phases of project management.

Enta Da Stage: The Initiating Phase

Projects shouldn't be confused with steady, recurring activities at work. Projects last only for a certain amount of time and have a beginning, middle, and end. They exist in every kind of commercial activity: developing a new manufacturing real-time monitoring software program, opening an overseas sales distribution office, recording and releasing an R. Kelly album, or launching a successful Kickstarter for the Grilled Cheesus, the sandwich iron to sear the Lord and Savior into your next panini. No matter what it is, they all start with the blandly named Project Initiation Phase. The intent during initiation is to imagine how the project is going to be when it is done; what is part of the job, and what doesn't belong. To get it going, project managers begin making a written charter that captures the project's deliverables, defines the scope of work, and figures out how to integrate the different task elements. These establish expectations for everyone involved in or affected by the endeavor and set the project up for success.

The deliverables are the things that the business will have or turn over to customers. With most projects, these are easy to identify. They can be concrete things like a clothing product for sale, a refurbished classic muscle car, or an operational Death Star. Deliverables may also include intangible things like market intelligence, research for search algorithms, or faster customer-service-response times. The exercise to record deliverables in the project charter commits the team to a clear outcome against which success can be measured. Project managers should always discuss the deliverable in the charter with stakeholders. It is a good way to make sure that everyone shares the same expectations about what a project is going to do or to make changes before the project gets too far down the road.

When Jay Rubin and Russell Simmons each threw in a few thousand dollars to become partners together at Def Jam Recordings, they started a business that would have a long series of projects, with Hip-Hop acts that altered the worldwide musical landscape. Although they never created formal written charters in keeping with the traditions of project management, they instinctively knew what had to come out of their work with the artists they signed to the label, like Run-DMC, LL Cool J, and the Beastie Boys. Rubin and Simmons could tell you the deliverables. There were tangible things like the albums, which they hoped would go gold, platinum, or better. There were the concert tours to showcase the new music. Of course, Simmons and Rubin expected to make money off the music. Then there were the intangible deliverables: an enhanced reputation for Def Jam Recordings, fan entertainment and customer satisfaction, and the creation of a vibrant new Hip-Hop culture that would change the world. No one ever said that project deliverables had to be modest.

Once the team knows the deliverables, they can create the project scope, which is the work that has to be done to supply the products, services, or functions. Breaking up the project into smaller elements ensures that each one can be detailed with its unique requirements and to reduce the risk that key pieces will be left out. In a building project, design, permitting, site work, foundation, electrical, plumbing, structural framing, roofing, and finishing are all individual parts of the larger project. Each one needs to be defined well enough to make the final product work the way it is supposed to. The scope should be detailed enough to allow an outside contractor the ability to provide a quote to do the job. Clarity in the work is super important when using third-party service providers since changes to the scope almost always drive up the cost.

For Black Entertainment Television (better known by its moniker BET), every Hip-Hop awards show is its own project. Consequently, the managers and editors break up each event into its constituent parts to define a scope of work that allows the station's staff to concentrate on their individual pieces. A team has to organize the industry insiders and fan input to gather nominees and select award winners. Another group has to arrange the venue with all of the complexity that goes with that—such as permits, security, decoration, seating arrangements, deposits, insurance, and audiovisual setup. Missing something in the scope here could cause some embarrassing on-air gaffes, and someone's head is likely to roll after that. The financial costs of the show require the development of a firm budget as well as advertising sales to offset the expenses and turn a profit. After all, BET wasn't doing the show for its health. Then there are the guest invitations, RSVPs, and artist-and-guest reception after their arrival. News flash: artists can be high maintenance. All of this is just the tip of the iceberg. The scope of work can and should go into much greater depth to make sure that when Hip-Hop's elite set foot onto the red carpet and the cameras roll, everything looks good, satisfies the viewers and guests, and leaves BET with a little more jingle in its pockets than it had before.

Projects are almost always large enough to make it necessary for a lot of parts to come together to make it happen. The way that project managers do that is through integration management. It is the process of prioritizing and coordinating the different parts of the projects to get to the final product. Life comes with enough friction that things don't always go according to plan— bad weather, sickness, scheduling conflicts, equipment lead time, development delays, etc. When that happens, managers make trade-offs with the various elements during integration to meet or exceed the expectations that the project stakeholders have. The best project managers are able to make integration appear seamless, but it is generally a result of good coordination and communication within the project team and with the contractors doing part of the work. Although integration starts during the initiation phase, it continues throughout all the phases until completion.

To create a single, someone has to write the lyrics. Another person has to make the beats. Then the artists have to actually perform the track, which requires scheduling equipment and studio time. Even then there is still the polishing and editing, and unless the music is just art for art's sake, the song has to be promoted and released. Those have to be completed in a particular order, and they have to come together just right to make the hit that the fan base, the artists, and the record label all expect.

In the NPR radio program "Planet Money: *How Much Does It Cost to Make a Hit Song?*" Zoe Chase explains how the labels integrate the moving parts of musical production to create a single.

> *At a writing camp, a record label hires the best music writers in the country and drops them into the nicest recording studios in town for about two weeks. It's a temporary version of the old music-industry hit factories, where writers and producers cranked out pop songs.*[1]

The individual writers will create song after song, some which will be used in one form or another on a single or album and others which never see the light of day. In some cases, writers don't even see the artists. Top-tier rappers aren't scribbling lyrics on notepads in their homes, on the street, or in garages in the way they did before they were famous. The products that the writers generate are combined with the work of producers, vocal producers, audio technicians, managers, promoters, distributors, and lawyers to deliver the goods. Each person's individual contributions are important to the ultimate success of the music, and project managers must know how to integrate all of the pieces to generate the hits.

The Blueprint: The Planning Phase

Project planning is the second phase and most difficult in a project's life cycle. It takes many of the products generated in the initiation phase and formalizes them into actionable strategies. The team creates a set of plans to direct activities through execution, monitoring and control, and final closure of the project. The more work that project teams do during the planning phase, the better the chances are for success. Plans help the team to manage risks, time, cost, quality, and the deviations that pop up throughout the project. Some of the things that project managers need to plan are resources, costs, and time estimates. Planning should strike a balance between activities that must occur and contingency planning that gives the project some flexibility when things inevitably start to change.

If the plans of a project are like a recipe, then the resources required are the ingredients. Determining what and how much is necessary to do the job is the crux of the resource plan. It should call out the types and amount of labor required, especially where skill sets are hard to come by, expensive, or are unclear. Most projects need some kind of equipment to reach the finish line, such as computers, construction equipment, or special-use deep-sea submersible vehicles. On the way to building a cost plan, the project needs an estimate for the total materials required to get the job done. If you need it, the resource plan should have it listed. When it came to Hip-Hop, Dre knew what ingredients he needed to add as part of his plan.

Dr. Dre's rise to prominence in Hip-Hop was a sort of project unto itself. There was the know-how he and his crew would need during performances to keep the crowd jumping. The clubs in L.A. at the time he was coming up required performers to look good, so that meant they would need costumes. In addition to practicing to do covers of other bands' music, Dre's group would need to make its own music, and that meant writing their own lyrics and mixing their own beats. But for Dre, who claimed his doctor's title for "mixology," the most important thing that would appear on the resource plan was his equipment and the skill to use it.

Dre had started out tearing apart old stereo equipment to create homemade mixing equipment.[2] Once he had something—speakers, tape decks, turntables, amplifiers—he'd spend hours learning how to squeeze every decibel of sound out of it. Dre placed greater and greater value on music equipment, and he knew that the equipment required training to make it useful.

And when [Dre's friend] kept getting better equipment—a bigger board, an eight track, and soon a twelve-track— Dre kept teaching himself the dynamics of the songwriting and production, amassing a collection of beats and searching for a way out.[3]

The planning phase of Dr. Dre's rise to power might not have been as strictly prescribed as project management's bible, *The Project Management Body of Knowledge*, but the resources he and his partners would need could very easily have been catalogued in a resource plan.

Projects live and die by the money it takes to finish. Cost management plans and controls a project's budget with financing, estimating, budgeting, managing, and controlling. Project sponsors, the people who write the checks and set the limits on total costs, expect managers to watch the till and keep expenses under control. Their hope is that the team will get the job done within the budget. The project manager needs to use the resources list and the scope of work to quote jobs with contractors, cost out the purchase of materials, factor in labor, and estimate costs based on similar, previously completed projects. Once the team has crunched the numbers, the budgets should be reviewed with the sponsors. There are times when it is better to ask for forgiveness than permission, but when a project manager is just trying to establish trust with the sponsors is not a good one. Cost management runs throughout the life of the project, since costs, like everything else, can change as time goes by.

Oliver "Power" Grant was one of the founding members who worked with RZA to make the Wu-Tang Clan into a Hip-Hop sensation. Their plan had a number of aspects. There were the human-resource solutions to create a diverse cast of artists and affiliated bands. Wu-Tang spread the group out to several record labels for risk mitigation. And for greater promotion, improved name recognition, and a bit more skrilla, the Wu-Tang Clan created Wu-Wear, its own branded clothing line.

In the beginning, Power paid a guy $100 to sneak into a silk-screen shop after hours to add the iconic Wu-Tang "W" trademarks to shirts.[4] Once they realized how strong the demand for Wu-Wear was, RZA and Power figured out what it would take to move the brand to the next level. There was the cost of Linden, the West Indian tailor RZA and Power hired to sew camouflage fabric into clothes and add Wu-Wear tags into merchandise. There was the cost of the materials to make the clothes themselves. And there was the cost of the new store to serve as their point of sales.

> ... the new Wu-Wear store [was] on 61 Victory Boulevard in Staten Island, halfway between the Stapleton Projects and the ferry at St. George Terminal. The shelves of the eight-hundred-square-foot boutique were laden with caps, shorts, shirts, jerseys.[5]

All told, Power spent $50,000 to stock the store. In this case, Power and the Wu-Tang Clan had most of the things that they needed to make a cost management plan, and that may have contributed to the fact that Wu-Wear sold well for a long time after its introduction.

After project sponsors tell the project manager how much money they are willing to spend, they usually follow up by asking when it will be done. To give needy sponsors the honest answers that they demand, project managers need accurate time estimates for the work to be done. Smart project managers will do what they can to keep stakeholders clued in on timing throughout the assignment. The estimates drive planning and delivery deadlines. Timing is affected by the availability of supplies, weather, contractor progress, permit timing, advances or snags in research, and even team members' lame staycations with family. Seriously. Where are your priorities, dude? Get back to work.

Revenge can be a project, too, and timing is a big part of any plan to seek vengeance. In 2006, Cristal champagne had a reputation for being the gold standard for high-end bubbly. From the exclusive ski resorts of Davos, Switzerland, to the mansions of Hollywood, the world's rich enjoyed sipping their $450 to $600 cuvées. It wasn't surprising, then, that the Hip-Hop set wanted to have some of that cachet and exclusivity rub off on them when enjoying Cristal at the clubs, private parties, and even while showcasing the brand in videos. A businessperson might have thought that the arrangement was a win-win for the Hip-Hop set and Louis Roederer, the parent company that produced Cristal. But that is probably because the average businessperson has better sense than Frederic Rouzaud, the empty-headed managing director of Louis Roederer.

When asked by reporters from *The Economist* what he thought of Rap artists showing so much public affection for Cristal, Rouzaud replied, "That's a good question, but what can we do? We can't forbid people from buying it. I'm sure Dom Perignon or Krug would be delighted to have their business."[6] The racist gaffe sent the Hip-Hop community into a rage with widespread boycotts of Cristal, and Jay-Z in particular decided to take the fight to Louis Roederer by launching his own competing champagne.

Jay-Z sought out French champagne vintner, Cattier, to create an exclusive brand of champagne that he could sponsor. Cattier and Jay-Z essentially created Armand de Brignac to capitalize on the Cristal boycott. Before the product could be sold in American clubs, Cattier would need to figure out when grapes could be cultivated and processed. Suppliers needed to create and deliver the new and distinctive Armand de Brignac packaging, and then there was the timing of the promotion of the new brand when it was finally ready for sale. The project to stick it to Frederic Rouzaud was successful (and wildly profitable for Jay-Z and Cattier) in part because the timing of their revenge champagne was well managed to get the product out to replace Cristal.[7]

Capital Punishment: The Executing Phase

The work gets underway during execution, the third phase in project management. The deliverables start to take shape . . . or at least on ones that have a physical aspect to them, and the promise of completion starts to come into view. The customers start to think of signoff and final acceptance of the project. The only thing left to do is . . . everything, actually. Project managers still need to oversee procurement, deal with changes, and monitor quality. Murphy's Law dictates that the third-party suppliers you hired to do critical work and deliver materials in a timely manner will drop the ball. It's probably not even your fault, but it happens. The project team will constantly have to juggle issues in procurement and scheduling snafus. The changes that life throws at projects will need similar mental flexibility. Vagaries associated with the endeavor promise to upend all of the carefully laid plans created with so much hope and optimism in the innocent days of the planning phase. Project managers who are able to keep suppliers on track and prevent changes from blowing up the budget or the timeline will still have to keep an eye on the quality of project elements. Yep, executing will keep you jumping.

The project probably wouldn't be going anywhere without purchasing goods and services from outside organizations. There are many tools available to project managers when dealing with contractors, but the three most useful are contract writing, relationships, and payments. Each one can and should be used to keep the goods and services the project needs flowing. Contracts are the formal instruments calling out the legal obligations all parties have to the project. Prior to agreeing to work with any contractor, managers should quote jobs with at least three competing firms. This gives the company a mix of price and service offerings to choose from. A little research with industry groups or even Google searches can determine what the customary terms are for most kinds of contracts. Project managers should feel empowered to push for better terms, such as timing, quality, or price in contracts prior to signing. Once the contract is in place, all parties have their playbook . . . in theory.

Relationships can go a long way to working through procurement troubles, or they can make a bad situation worse. Contractors are like every other business on the planet. If they don't have to work hard to maintain business, they won't. Project managers can use a contractor's desire to continue to work with the company on future projects as a carrot to get better, faster, and cheaper services. Project team members can also build rapport with the contractors and use their connections to get more from suppliers. Conversely, poor relationships at the company, with the manager, or at the team level can be a detriment to the project, and project managers should work to keep relations professional, if not friendly.

The last tool is the most effective in certain ways: payment control. Contracts and relationships are great bonds between contractors and the company, but behind it all is everyone's desire for money. A project manager should always hold some portion of payments to contractors as leverage to ensure that outside suppliers do what they agree to. Paying too early makes negotiating much more difficult when things aren't right. Why would a contractor do anything when they got what they came for: your cash? Less frequently used (but still useful) payment control tools include early payment and bonus offerings for outstanding service, but use these very carefully. Money withheld is usually a more effective motivator than early or extra money.

When you want to see how *not* to do something in project management, you can always count on DMX to help out. From his inability to conceptualize and plan through to his sloppy execution and control, X didn't ever have to worry about closing out projects. They usually ended badly, without much hope for a sequel. When our story takes place, DMX was splitting his time evenly between third-rate criminal activity and amateur rapping. To his credit, he was getting some notoriety for his performances in clubs. One day while DMX was abusing his dog after he may or may not have killed a neighborhood cat, a local promoter, Jack MacNasty, approached him with a proposition to be his manager.

> *I liked Jack. I trusted him . . . He was more like an older brother to me than a manager, so I had no hesitation in signing his paperwork. But soon after I did, I realized that what I had just done was going to keep me broke for a long time.*[8]

Despite the title of rapper, DMX didn't have an album or a record deal with a label; and, unfortunately for him, there were only two minor companies with lukewarm interest in him. Without realizing it, DMX obligated himself to cover his own extensive expenses, with no means to pay for them. He would have to cover the considerable costs of his time in the studio, production, and engineering without any help from his good friend, Jack MacNasty.

DMX managed to violate every rule of procurement management from contract to relationship and on through payment control. Three quotes, man! Get three quotes for a job, especially when you've never done it previously!! And for God's sake, read and understand the contract *before* you sign!!! Additionally, whenever there is a question as to which weighs more—the relationship with a nearly unknown acquaintance with a monetary interest in you or the contract—err on the side of the legally binding and enforceable document and less on the sketchy creep salivating over you with dollar signs in his eyes. Good relations are great, but they can crumble fast when money gets involved. Lastly, there is payment. Sometimes it is better to hold off on expenses until a definite revenue stream emerges to cover costs, and definitely don't agree to let someone else get paid before you know when and how you get yours. Come on, X. Get with the program.

Projects are made up of people, processes, and technology, and all of them can defy plans and expectations. Change management is how project managers cope with deviations from the plan. The process is like so many others: identify the problem, recognize the ultimate project goal, and act to achieve the goal or cut your losses.

Identifying the problem can be easy. Key personnel can win the lottery, get sick, quit, retire, get promoted, or die all without the project manager's permission. Weather, economic forces affecting corporate sales, supplier control systems, and even seeming certainty of steady US postal delivery can all change without notice. Technology, too, offers little to no continuity. Machine parts can go obsolete. Artificial Intelligence promises to disrupt whole industries, and companies can refuse to support old software just when you need assistance most.

Managers who know what's changed have to see how it relates to the project goals. The tsunami that struck East Asia in 2011 disrupted global supply chains, forcing project managers to seek alternative components for auto parts, medical devices, and even Hello Kitty paraphernalia. A tidal wave of corporate defaults affecting your company might make the holiday-party-planning project you're working on irrelevant as security escorts everyone from the building. The manager's role is to understand to what degree changes alter the project's overall outcome.

50 Cent's mission to start up a semi-autonomous point of sale for illegal narcotics had lots of hallmarks that project managers would recognize. He had project goals and knew the work he had to do to succeed. He was smart enough not to write them down at the time, but 50 had his firm but flexible plans. So when his business environment transformed, Curtis Jackson fell back on good change management.

Dealing in Southside Queens wasn't ever legal, but there was a pattern to the back-and-forth between police and dealers. Police usually couldn't do much if dealers were smart enough to stash drugs in trash on the street, have someone else carry, or use broken pay phones . . . anywhere other than on their person. How could the cops prove possession if a dealer wasn't in *possession* at the time of arrest? In that environment, business took place following certain conventions.

The police Tactical Narcotics Team, called TNT, changed all of that. Where arrests had been individually targeted, the TNT swept into an area and rounded up everyone from kingpins to innocent bystanders. They would establish a relationship between people holding and those they suspected of dealing to create cases that would hold up in police-friendly courts. The rules of the game had changed.

50 recognized that the TNT strategy meant that dealing would be more challenging, but arrest had always been a risk. This particular kind of aggressive policing could still be mitigated to stand up the dealership. Rather than relying on kids to hold product who might be just as likely to get rounded up during a TNT sweep, 50 decided to start carrying his own stash on his person and trust his legs to keep him out of police custody. "In the event that a dealer had to run, at least he would be running with his inventory on him."[9] Problem partially solved. Who said that change management had to be complicated?

People remember the quality of a thing even after they've forgotten the price, so maintaining quality throughout a project is a good way to ensure project success. Professionals should still hold up a high-quality standard even for jobs where things are being done with tight budgets and lower-grade materials. A customer might not want to pay for premium gasoline, but they still expect a gas engine car to work when they put in 85 octane. The products and services that the team hands over at the end have to meet quality levels agreed to during initiation. The better the project goes, the more likely the company is to do well, and the more likely the manager and team are to be rewarded. Making sure that the deliverables meet standards, the project team can use quality specifications, regular inspection, and controls to correct discrepancies.

The project team should establish quality specifications for deliverables in coordination with the sponsors and stakeholders during initiation, and they should reconfirm them during contracting in the planning phase. The specifications can be as detailed or general as is necessary. Regardless, the standard should be clear enough to allow the people responsible for the work to prepare and execute the tasks to meet the specifications. The quality records should be made in a way that they could be handed off to new personnel or another contractor without having to reinvent the wheel.

Soviet, Iraqi, and Iranian arms-control agreements were all based on the concept of "Trust, but verify." Western governments demanded the ability to inspect sites to ensure that no government was engaged in nefarious nonsense with weapons of mass destruction. The stakes might be lower on your typical business project than in strategic arms control, but inspection and verification are valuable tools to maintain quality standards on jobs. Where project team members are capable of it, they should conduct reviews of progress on deliverables using the quality specifications. If no one on the team is qualified to do verification, project managers should arrange for third-party inspections on critical points.

Quality controls are the remedial actions that the project team and outside contractors will take to bring parts of the project back into the limits set in the specifications. Think of patching a ding in a car door, replacing damaged tiles in a kitchen, or reprogramming code to eliminate an annoying, unexpected error. Contracts should include clauses describing who is responsible for costs associated with errors and rework. Where items are not included in contract language or the specifications, the project manager will need to negotiate to correct quality defects with internal suppliers or outside contractors. Quality isn't easy, but it pays dividends.

Tariq "Black Thought" Trotter and Ahmir "Questlove" Thompson of The Roots worked hard at their craft, but, just as for anyone else, things didn't always go perfectly. Questlove told the story of an event in a club when he played a song that he knew was not ready for prime time. As he put it, no one booed him off the stage, but the lukewarm reception left Questlove feeling pretty rotten and would ultimately set a quality standard for The Roots.

> I knew from then on that anything I did had to meet the standard of the room. It wasn't enough to appeal to some unseen critics. I needed the artists around me to react with more than the straight-ahead, quiet-as-the-grave head bob.[10]

Similar to indie artists, The Roots inhabited a difficult commercial niche between garage bands and headliner acts. They were selling a few hundred thousand copies of their albums, but they were not breaking into gold, let alone platinum, record certifications, a level that would have ensured solid interest from labels, critics, and fans. The Hip-Hop duo wisely asked themselves some good questions about quality.

> *We were making music that mattered to us, but we needed to know that it mattered to anyone else—or, if it didn't, why not. The fact that we were somehow falling short was a source of consternation . . . Was there something we were doing wrong? . . . Were we coming up short in the entertainment department or long in the substance department? Either one of those things could affect a record's sales.*[11]

The Roots and their sponsors at record labels like DCG, Def Jam, and Interscope had certain minimum economic specifications to maintain, and those were measured by album sales. Black Thought and Questlove would experiment with styles and sounds until they found things that satisfied them and the fan base and that paid the bills. Their work on quality paid off with gold and platinum certifications for some albums and a number of awards for Best Performance by a Duo Group, Best Traditional R&B Vocal Performance, and Best R&B Album.

By All Means Necessary: The Monitoring and Control Phase

In the execution phase, cranes swung into place at construction sites, people compiled research for marketing reports, engineers wrote code for new programs, tailors stitched materials into designer clothes, environmental teams seeded grounds during remediation, and little-understood experiments proceeded forward at suspicious Swiss particle accelerators. Work during execution can be electrifying. There is slightly less sexy but equally important work to address during the monitoring and controlling phase. In it, the team oversees operations to keep the project on time, on budget, and within the specifications and metrics called out in the scope of work. The project team must compare the plan against actual results and make changes where necessary when things get off track. The monitoring and control phase has at its disposal many tools discussed previously: plans, quality, contracts, inspections, and integration management. Of equal importance is the management of human resources and communications.

Most projects are not the only thing going on in a company, and not everyone is going to be on the project team. Under those conditions, a business can be quickly divided into "us and them," the lit match among explosive materials of human relations. Properly managing staff (on and off the project team and inside and outside the company) is essential to getting through the unpredictable nature of project work and advancing your career.

Human resources are an important consideration from initiation through closing. In the early phases of a project, the team should decide on how to divide up roles and responsibilities among the people doing the work. Creating organization charts showing reporting relationships and staffing levels should be done at the same time in planning. The clearer and better understood the expectations are for project staffing by people both inside and outside the project, the lower the chances of conflicts over scheduling, priorities, and power grabbing. But after the organizing and socializing of a human resources plan is complete, the project manager still has some heavy lifting to do with personnel, namely training, scheduling, and engagement.

Some projects have the benefit of highly experienced, veteran project team members. Others are staffed by people so new and green a team leader might wonder who kidnapped the kindergarten class and why they brought them to work. In both cases, there is a certain amount of training that a project manager needs to arrange for things to go smoothly. The human resource plan that broke out the reporting relationships, roles, and responsibilities is a guide that should highlight what skills are needed to do the job and what skills the available staff actually has. The difference between what expertise and proficiency are needed and what is available is the basis for a project's training plan.

The minimum training a team should have contains administrative and organization familiarization and basic workplace safety. The familiarization training should get the team acquainted with one another and their parts in the project. The safety training is important to set a tone on the job that will send workers home with all of their limbs intact. Bad workplace safety is a great way to needlessly run up project costs, injure workers, and open the company and contractors up to legal action. Other specialized training on special skills that team members or contractor staff need can be arranged either using experienced staff or through third-party trainers. The Department of Labor has some free training programs available. Local colleges and schools may offer other pay-for-service courses that might be useful. However, if generalized training is not available, Internet searches for specialized training can turn up a program match quickly.

Dana Elaine "Queen Latifah" Owens grew up in a respectable, middle-class, musically inclined family in New Jersey; but while her supportive family life gave her many advantages, it did not give her the skills she was going to need to become a rapper. At the time her interest in Hip-Hop started, the music was only just taking off. Clubs in the various boroughs of New York City had new acts all the time, and Latifah and her brother would go to party and check things out. It wasn't long before she decided that she wanted to be one of the people up on the stage, but it wasn't like there were government training programs or community college courses teaching people how to make it in Hip-Hop. Some training is just too specialized.

Instead, Latifah and her brother engaged in their own home-made self-education.

*We had every Rap album and every Hip-Hop magazine—
all two of them.* Right On! *and* Word-Up *gave us the low-
down on who was releasing a record, who had just been
signed to a deal . . . We wanted to know everything we
could about the artists, the music, the clothes. We studied
Rap inside and out . . . we knew what we were getting
ourselves into. It was like the training before the job.*[12]

It was not quick, but the lessons that Latifah and her brother
learned over time through their reading and discussions put them
in a good position when the opportunity came for her to get
into the Rap game. There weren't many surprises for her when
she performed, and she made fewer mistakes than many young
artists new to the industry with managers, contracts, and the
administrative challenges that occur behind the scenes. Latifah's
example is a good reminder to project managers that training
does not have to be fancy to be effective and that there is a way
to learn about subjects that aren't always easily accessible. You
just have to have the will to make it happen.

Projects often have to share personnel with the non-project
parts of the company doing the regular job and keeping the lights
on. Even when there are no organizational conflicts, scheduling
is a test of a project manager's talent. Everyone has commitments
and claims on their time whether they want them or not; sick
kids, project meetings, training events, work deadlines, aging
parents, sales calls, vendor conferences, weddings, traffic court,
vacations, and funerals. Some things people can control, others
they can't.

People enjoy having some stability at work, and the schedule
can provide that. Early warning on events gives people a chance
to prepare for them mentally and strategically. The more complicated and specialized the material, the more time people generally
need for preparation. Managers can score big points with team

members by making scheduling decisions and notifying people well in advance of events. And managers can spend those points on emergency events when there is little or no time to prepare a response. A manager can give a little to get a lot.

Even for specialized entertainment companies like Live Nation, concert tours are probably one of the most challenging projects from a scheduling perspective. A single, modest Hip-Hop concert with Lauryn Hill, Nas, Noname, Little Simz, and Kehlani can sell out a venue for between 2,000 and 5,000 fans. In 2016, that required dozens of security personnel, ticket takers and ushers, A/V engineers, teamsters, agents, lawyers, electricians, carpenters, supervisors, sound technicians, drivers, and we haven't even mentioned the musicians, entourage, and headline artists. Coordinating the activities, conflicting priorities, and general chaos that went with a few hundred people was a daunting task.

The team leader had to organize the staff to break up the numbers into something manageable with a hierarchy that allowed a few people to manage much larger groups. The project team had to ensure that venue preparations continued on schedule with lights, power, decoration, sound, and video. Managers had to ensure that their people were prepared to do their jobs when they were needed or find others to do the job when there was the inevitable fallout of vacations, firings, sick calls, resignations, or no-shows.

On the night of the concert, the stage manager had to shuffle acts and artists on and off stage, and those artists have their own ideas about time and schedules. Once the last encore had been played, the project manager still had to pack up the talent and staff and move them to the hotel or off to the next show. Oh, and there was still the little matter of coordinating the teardown and collecting payments at the last gig. Multiply this ritual by 20 or 30 shows, and you get the sense that scheduling was a life-or-death matter in project management. And with all due respect to Lauryn Hill and Nas, these weren't even the biggest acts in Hip-Hop. Maybe there was a good reason for all those drugs on the tour bus.

Of course, project team members have to be trained and scheduled. No project manager is surprised by that. Engaging people is a more nebulous but vital aspect to human resources. It is the sum of all professional exchanges, casual interactions, and disciplinary encounters that take place during the course of the assignment. Project managers have to navigate a wide range of human interactions from dull lulls in activity to high-stress operational emergencies and from obscenity-filled exchanges with enraged contractors to alcohol-fueled holiday parties with the staff. Engaged managers are more likely to know about and be able to react to growing risks and opportunities because of the open communication they maintain and the trust it creates.

There is no such thing as perfect engagement. People react differently to all kinds of interactions, but attributes like honesty, positivity, and regular contact seem to have a lot of upside. A manager's people want to know that what they hear from her is true and that they aren't having their chain yanked needlessly. Leaders shouldn't blow smoke at the team just to dress up a bad situation, but maintaining a positive attitude can have a wider, constructive effect. Employees are inclined to work harder in upbeat environments, and managers have outsized influences on the atmosphere. Introverts cringe at the thought, but connecting with team members is essential to good engagement. Relationships require care and feeding, and that means meeting the team where they are. Occasionally that is exchanging texts or getting out of the office to talk.

Leila Steinberg was a young, well-connected music promoter who was in the right place at the right time to take on Tupac Shakur at the start of his career. She used her family contacts to establish and cultivate relationships in the entertainment business. Additionally, she created an afterschool program in the same area where the mid-'90s Rap god lived that attracted hundreds of kids from all kinds of different linguistic, racial, and cultural backgrounds. The workshops focused on writing and performance that were good springboard opportunities into the next level on the Bay Area Hip-Hop scene.

> *If you were part of the underground Bay Area Hip-Hop scene and wanted to hit the big time, you had to impress the White Girl of Hip-Hop. If you wanted a record deal, Leila was a person to get to know.*[13]

Leila was good enough to know talent when she heard it, and when Tupac took up the mic at her auditions, he blew her away with his content, delivery, and rhyming. She recognized that he was raw and would need some polishing. For example, Tupac was a bit of a slob, preferring to buy new clothes rather than wash the dirty ones he already owned.[14] Leila was smart enough to know that there were some things that she couldn't control and decided that Pac's personal hygiene was maybe a bridge too far. Instead she focused on his performance. She earned Tupac's trust, and her focus and dedication got him his first record deal with Interscope.

Leila was a great example of how engaging people in and around a project can have very positive results. Kids in Marin City got a chance to learn about performing arts. Clubs and record companies got access to hot new acts, which helped them keep their edge and relevance to their customers. And Tupac Shakur found a friend and mentor who helped launch him and Hip-Hop into a new chapter in music history. Leila certainly wouldn't have been able to do that hiding in her office.

Every part of business requires communication in order to succeed, so it is no surprise that project management needs it, too. Communications management helps keep the stakeholders informed and happy. Well . . . that is a high bar to set. Let's settle for keeping stakeholders informed and less than totally furious. Consulting with people who care about some part of the project gives people a chance to express their concerns, vent their frustrations, or even provide valuable guidance just in time to save the day.

There are lots of means to get a message across to people: semaphore, smoke signals, and emojis. A project manager should never hesitate to use whatever means are practical to convey a message because the free flow of information is so important to the success of the project. However, when planning for steady-state communications, there are a few tried-and-true methods to keep the people who need to know in the loop. The most traditional means are regular reports and meetings.

Reports might be painful to read and even more painful to write. So why go to all that trouble? Good reports are meant to keep you out of trouble by getting facts into the hands of the people who need them, and that material can drive decisions that keep the project on track. They can be as short as a single paragraph, issued almost daily, or voluminous, going on for chapters, released once or twice a year. The length, detail, and timing of reports depend entirely on who needs what information, but the structure of a report can be the key to conveying information relatively quickly and cleanly.

In our world of serious attention deficit and hyperactivity disorders, project teams who can get to the point quickly are going to be more successful than those that prattle on and on and on and on . . . There are a few ways to cut to the chase fast: the executive summary, topic sentences, and conclusions and recommendations. The executive summary is a quick rundown of the main points in the account that you put at the very beginning of the report. If you can put together a short summary that makes further reading largely unnecessary, you're a hero.

Time-saving technique number two is the topic sentence. Many reports will require lots of detail. A topic sentence leading off any given paragraph serves as a summary of the information that follows. A good topic sentence does for the reader on a small scale what the executive summary does for the whole report. Readers will dive into the details of the paragraph if they are interested, or they will be able to move along quickly if they aren't.

Lastly, a report needs conclusions and recommendations. This is the part of the end of the report that gives the reader a roundup of the material and the action items that the team or stakeholders have to address. It should be short and to the point, with only a bare minimum of detail to drive home the message. This material should also be highlighted in the executive summary.

If, in the early days, Hip-Hop was a project to create a new sound and scene, *The Source* was how it was reported to the world. The magazine even adopted the slogan "The Voice of the Rap Music Industry."[15] It started as a local periodical in Boston, but as Hip-Hop's popularity spread, its stakeholders' demand for information about it increased, too. Those stakeholders were the artists, fans, and industry types. They were anyone who cared about the new music coming out of clubs, house parties, and increasingly recognized record labels. *The Source* tried hard to give people content that entertained and informed in each edition. There were record sales charts, featurettes on Rap radio DJs, and coverage of new acts. All of it was useful information to the different groups of readers.

The Source didn't do much in the way of an executive summary of the wide-ranging content included in each publication. Its writers were never fans of the academic-style topic sentence in their prose, but the magazine did have conclusions and recommmendations peppered throughout in the form of editorial content. The effect of *The Source's* reporting was to inform and entertain the audience, and it promoted some artists, styles, and sounds, and looked over others. Ultimately, it created part of the Hip-Hop culture that is so well established today, and that is a sign of effective project reporting.

Almost any movie about mobsters includes the stereotypical scene of gangsters meeting in smoke-filled back rooms. Did you ever wonder why that is? Well, love them or hate them, meetings are a valuable tool to keep communication flowing in an organization or on a project. Reports provide collaborators and associates some flexibility as to when or even if they read the information. Meetings provide a more direct, dynamic, and interactive connection between participants, and that can be worth a lot. As with crime families hashing out beefs over territory, illegal-racket grievances, or barroom beatings, regular sit-downs can update team members, manage change, establish new paths forward, and/or clear the air over the untimely demise of "made" men under suspicious circumstances.

Project meetings fall into three categories: regular, special, and ad hoc. Regular meetings take place on some kind of schedule: quarterly, monthly, weekly, daily . . . whatever frequency that they need to be to exchange the information to move the job along. These are great for humdrum information that is updated only occasionally. Project managers should call special meetings if and when there is a larger, specific subject that can be defined and addressed with a select group of participants but which doesn't belong as part of regular-meeting discussion. There should be enough time to plan, prepare, and invite attendees for special meetings. On the other hand, project teams can throw together ad hoc meetings with all the planning and foresight of a late-night visit to Waffle House. The topics usually can't be very complex or wide ranging since it is hard to gather the information necessary to resolve. Ad hoc meetings are good for small issues that require input from only a few people.

When you add up the time, effort, and wages of the people involved, meetings are expensive. There are a few other rules that make meetings less painful that project managers should bear in mind.

1. A clear purpose that the attendees understand.
2. A list of invitees that includes everyone who needs to be there (but does not needlessly include a cast of thousands).
3. Start and end at fixed times.
4. Set a location even if that location is cyberspace or a conference call.
5. Stick to the agenda.

These techniques can keep meetings mercifully short and productive by focusing the group on addressing the issues that need attention. Anything else would just be a very poor excuse for a party.

After 50 Cent had established himself in the Rap game, he decided to start his own crew of performers, G-Unit. Crews gave marquee artists an opportunity to boost their own brand while promoting other, less well-known artists. The top-billing rapper appeared on more music, thereby keeping his or her name alive, and the crew artists got additional attention from their mentor's star power. In theory, the setup was a win-win for everyone involved, but things weren't going according to 50's plan. The team members weren't pulling their weight.

50 Cent decided to regulate in one of the most baller special meetings in the recorded history of Hip-Hop. An awestruck Prodigy of Mobb Deep recounted the story. 50 had G-Unit meet at his offices with Young Buck on speakerphone. He went through the list of issues: broken album-release timelines, cost overruns on personal maintenance, family problems, artist absenteeism, lost

revenue, and low profits. 50 had an agenda to point out weaknesses in the performance of his team. He allowed time for the attendees to reply and engage. He remained in charge, directing the conversation where it needed to go, and when it was over, everyone knew what they had to do. And that is how it's done . . .

Death Certificate: The Closing Phase

With talent, hard work, and luck, projects will eventually come to an end. Closing is the last phase, and it is intended to wrap up the loose ends of the job and hand over the finished product to the customer. On any large assignments, there are plenty of things that need to be finished in the final stages: documentation and final reports, reassigning team members, concluding supplier contracts, site cleanup, and lots of bottle popping at the last party. Although not exclusive to the closing phase, project managers have to address risk management on the job and have a plan to deal with participants and interested parties. If first impressions are important to get work off to a good start, a strong finish on a project goes a long way to smoothing out the bumps people felt along the road, erase unpleasant memories, and set the team up for successful future projects. The close-out leaves customers and partners with feelings that will result in positive or negative reviews, so don't spike the ball in the end zone too early.

Project teams should use the checklists, contracts, and plans created early in the assignment for finalization work. The original documents and communications agreeing to changes to the scope of work can ensure that the team dots all the i's and crosses all the t's by detecting things that may have been missed in the thrash of execution. There is almost always documentation and other paperwork that accompany any finished product, and teams that don't keep up with it throughout the job will find updating it before completion painful. Teams will need to inspect suppliers' work before allowing final payments. If something needs to be corrected, closing is the time to get it fixed. Once the last payment goes out the door, a team's leverage with contractors goes with it. The work in the final phase should leave most people with a sense of closure.

When N.W.A. broke up in 1991, it left a hole in the Hip-Hop world. They had been the most popular group on the scene in no small part because of their raw, in-your-face lyrics, which got their music banned from many music outlets; and their unrepentantly urban and criminal image gave light to a little-examined corner of American society. Fans still remember their cutting-edge sound and hardcore image that made them and Gangsta Rap famous. After the breakup, the individual rappers of the group went out into the world to do other things. In the case of Ice Cube, Eazy-E, and Dr. Dre, those other things propelled them onto higher heights in the entertainment industry. Departing when they did probably helped cement their fame in keeping with the maxim that it is better to burn out than fade away.

Like so many great things of the past, fans always hoped for a return of N.W.A. Even though most of the remaining members of the group (Eazy-E having died in 1995) were amenable to the idea, Dr. Dre was the holdout opposed to the reunion. By the time that there was serious discussion of a get-together in 2004 and 2005, Dre had established himself as one of Hip-Hop's largest and most active icons. The idea of getting together with Arabian Prince, DJ Yella, and MC Ren (who needed Dre much more than Dre needed them) for a romp through the nearly defunct tracks of Gangsta Rap seemed more trouble than it was worth. The unfinished nature of the N.W.A. project seemed to continue for fans, but miracles do happen. Fortunately for fans, Ice Cube and the gang agreed to do a reunion at Coachella in 2016 in part to promote a major motion picture portrayal of their rise to fame, *Straight Outta Compton*. The reunion succeeded in paying respects to the band's roots, unite the group (or at least most of it) one last time, and break out music that brought Rap into the mainstream. That is pretty good project closure, but it would have been better with Dre there, too.

"Shit Happens" is probably the quickest way to summarize risk. Although people tend to think of risks as exclusively negative, like earthquakes, financial meltdowns, and/or STDs from that hookup you don't quite remember. But there are such things as positive risks like good weather, useful discoveries and breakthroughs, or an unexpected booty call with someone who is totally slamming. Good or bad, a team needs to manage the uncertainties they face throughout the life of a project. The process starts with identifying risk factors, analyzing the likelihood of their occurrence, and planning how to proactively respond if shit *actually* happens . . .

Every project has its risks, and it is up to the project manager and the team to recognize them early. When the team asks "what if" questions about the job, risk factors come to the surface. The team then has to decide how likely it is that risks will happen and what they are going to do about them. Construction and flight-testing projects can be severely affected by bad weather. Mergers between financial institutions can receive intrusive government scrutiny from the Securities and Exchange Commission. And the risks associated with robberies at high-end stores in greater L.A. make a very long list.

"I wasn't planning on getting locked up for a *week*, let alone hearing some judge handing me down a prison sentence with football numbers."[16] Ice-T knew that the robbery game was dangerous, and he ran his risk-management process with a healthy respect for the consequences. To ensure that the robbery was worth the chance of getting caught, Ice-T and an attractive female co-conspirator would dress up in designer clothes and case a jewelry store weeks in advance to be sure that the place had merchandise they wanted. Police were always a threat, and to mitigate the hazards they posed, Ice-T planned for a robbery to last no longer than five minutes, whether alarms were sounding or not. Finally, there was the getaway.

> *Without giving up too much game, the real trick to any crime is figuring out where you're going after you do it . . . you start where you want to end up, two blocks over, and you walk that path backward. That way, your escape route is your route to the lick.*

> *The getaway is actually more important than anything that happens during the robbery itself. If you practice your getaway, if you visualize yourself in the role of the person in hot pursuit of you, you're making sure that they can't follow this maze that you've created.*[17]

Now that is how you do risk management. Seriously, the Project Management Institute should give Ice-T an honorary Project Management Professional certification.

Anyone who has ever served a meal for friends or family with all their competing requests and demands knows all about stakeholder management. You might be one whiskey sour, gluten allergy, or prematurely empty box of pizza away from disaster at dinner. Anyone who has an interest in favor of or opposed to the work counts as an interested party, and developing positive relationships with the people who have some part in a project is vital to your sanity and the success of the job. A big part of it is managing stakeholder expectations, and that has a lot of overlap with the project communications plan and human resources.

The project manager needs to know the stakeholders well enough to know when and what to share. Categorizing the people based on their motivations, goals, and interests will drive how to treat different players. In high-risk or controversial projects, stakeholder management plans might look like an FBI task force's suspect map. The project team should prioritize stakeholders based on their influence on the project. The more power a stakeholder has, the more attention the team will need to pay to them. The team should use communications like reports, tours, meetings, or visits to keep them happy or at least safely on the sidelines.

Jay-Z started Roc-A-Fella Records as an accessory to his Rap career, but it quickly took over as his primary business focus. He knew that an artist's time in the spotlight is limited, but business can last a lifetime. Roc-A-Fella grew with Jay-Z's success and the rising fortunes of the artists he signed and mentored. Once the label had crossed a certain sales threshold, major record labels wanted a piece of the business, and Jay-Z looked to get money out of the company. In order to accomplish the buyout without upsetting the applecart, he had to deal with his stakeholders.

First, there were the other co-founders of Roc-A-Fella Records, Damon Dash and Kareem "Biggs" Burke. They had to agree to selling out interest in the company to record labels and accept changes in operations. Def Jam and Universal Music Group, the purchasing corporations, would expect a certain kind of return on investment and control over how Roc-A-Fella managed its business, and Jay-Z needed to convince them that this was a good deal for them. The artists on Roc-A-Fella wanted reassurances that their musical projects would continue forward under the new leadership, and they wanted to know how much involvement Jay-Z would have with them once he was even richer and more independent after the sale. Finally, there were the fans. Jay-Z couldn't easily communicate with the mass of Hip-Hop customers to get their input on the deal to give up partial control of Roc-A-Fella. As a result, he had to know the musical tastes of the fan base and be able to continue to offer what they wanted in the future.

The Roc-A-Fella team talked with one another and eventually found common ground. They worked with the other stakeholders to get the job done in a way that made most people happy. Communications varied from group to group with lawyers and senior leaders involved for some, face-to-face talks with others, and publicists and press releases for fans and industry followers. Def Jam and Universal got access to the artists, including and especially Jay-Z, and in return they offered the strength of their wide distribution networks to increase sales. Jay-Z and the Roc-A-Fella team remained in place to continue to find, develop, and promote the new talent that the customer base demanded while ensuring the sales that the labels needed.[18] Jay-Z and the Roc-A-Fella team handled stakeholder management so well that the label's sale was largely seamless.

THE WAYS OF DEAD PRESIDENTS: BUSINESS FINANCE

MONEY IS THE LIFEBLOOD FOR business, and without it, there won't be much activity. Most businesses require some kind of cash at startup and continuing operations whether it is for a store's rent, stocking inventory, buying equipment, paying wages, or entertaining your entourage. A leader needs to know how much money the business requires and how to get it when it is needed. Too many companies fail without sufficient funds to keep the heart pumping.

The Wu-Tang Clan was correct in saying "Cash Rules Everything Around Me." When RZA and Power created Wu-Wear, the wildly popular clothing and merchandise line, financing the business was a big deal. There were the costs of the T-shirts and sweatshirts, the silk-screening press, the camouflage cloth, the tailor to sew the materials, shipping, and ultimately the decorations and rent for the Wu-Wear store on Staten Island.

No matter how popular the Wu-Tang Clan was, there was no guarantee of success for Wu-Wear. Even the Beatles had famously tried and failed with their own clothing line. To cover their costs, RZA and Power counted on cash receipts from mail-in orders and sales at concerts and shows. While there was good profit margin on most products for sale, the Wu-Wear's cash flow meant that RZA and Power could never take finances for granted. There was a delicate balance for the business that they had to understand and maintain.

Building Blocks of Bank: Finance Fundamentals

People rarely if ever mention Calvin "Snoop Dogg" Cordozar in the same breath as John Maynard Keynes, Milton Friedman, or Fed Chairwoman Janet Yellen. But pushing past the stiff academic language of prominent economists, Snoop showed that he grasped many of the same theories at work in the market.

> *Experts are always talking about the economics of selling drugs, as if any n----- with a third-grade education couldn't figure out from jump the simplest law of supply and demand; if you got a supply of what everyone demands, that's all the economics you're ever going to need.*[1]

For Snoop these lessons were not imparted in some ivy-covered institution of higher learning or the polished skyscrapers of top-tier investment banks. Snoop learned economics in one of Hip-Hop's all-too-common entry-level employment: selling drugs.

> *Naturally, peddling crack or chronic or crank or shine or whatever else is getting folks where they want to get is going to pay you more than flipping fishwiches at McD's or sitting on your ass in a bullet-proof booth at a gas station, taking money through a slot.*[2]

Perhaps the language was crude, but the foundations of economic theory were there with Snoop and a lot of others just like him.

Recognizing where money comes from and goes to and why is vital to success in business. Knowing the broad concepts enables you, like Snoop, to identify them at work in your job and make decisions to improve your position. There are economic essentials applicable in the workplace, and we'll see Hip-Hop examples of how it all flows.

Finance is a pillar of economics, and interest rates and credit assessments are significant supporting structures of finance. People need money to do the things they want to do, and generally there is someone out there willing to loan that money for the right price. A percentage over and above the initial sum is interest. It is the mechanism that makes a loan prospect worthwhile for the person or institution financing it. In most cases, the risk is what determines the interest rate: low risk, lower interest; high risk, higher interest.

An agency determines what kind of credit to offer a borrower based on an estimation of risk for the loan. The easier a person or institution can pay back a debt, the lower the likelihood of default and the better the credit. If there is a higher threat of failure to pay a debt due to limited resources, lost revenues, or a crippling drug habit, the lower the creditworthiness. After all, who would lend money to someone who can't or won't give it back?

The model of credit and interest rates remains the same, whether they are countries like Greece trying to pay for state activities or just some dude on the street hustling . . .

In order to complete his degree at Louisiana State University, David "Dee-1" Augustine Jr. took out tens of thousands of dollars in student loans with the private lender Sallie Mae. Had Sallie known that Dee-1 would get an advance from his record label sufficient to pay off shortly after graduating, the lender might have been a little more merciful with the interest rates and payment plan that they offered him.

However, in the absence of foreknowledge of what would be a lucrative record deal, Sallie Mae loan officers looked at Dee-1 with cold, calculating eyes. They took into account his family's financial situation, Dee-1's requested loan amount, his degree plan, and school standing. They compared him to similar students in his demographic, established a risk category, and offered him money on terms that left Dee-1 scrounging month after month just to cover the minimum payments.

Dee-1 signed with RCA after graduating with a degree in business marketing, and unlike too many college students, he used his bonus to pay back his student loans in full. He celebrated the fulfillment of the Millennial dream with the single "Sallie Mae Back," a fitting anthem for his debt-ridden generation.

People make the financial systems and the marketplace move with their work, income, and spending. As a result, labor markets and participation rates have an outsized impact on the economy in general and on individual businesses in particular. Labor determines availability for hiring, wages, and even how much money consumers have to spend on goods and services.

When things are good, people can jump from job to job, demand higher salaries, and throw their money around on the town. The good times are characterized by low unemployment rates and high participation rates. In bad times, if a person has a job, they stay. If wages don't go up, they still stay. Alternative jobs are difficult to get or simply not available. Families and individuals get very tight fisted with their earnings because of the scarcity and uncertainty. However, these generalizations leave out a couple points. Not all jobs are created equal. There can be good times and bad times occurring simultaneously for different sectors of the labor market.

There are good reasons that Hip-Hop culture is sensitive to inequality. You can hear it in the angry lyrics of Jadakiss' "Hard Times," Naughty by Nature's "Everything's Gonna Be Alright," or Kanye West's "Spaceship." The artists can see that some people have it easy while they deal with dead-end or no jobs. Unfortunately, labor markets are driven by demand. There are frequently too many unskilled workers or too few vacancies to afford decent wages. The use of automation and offshoring of formerly safe middle-class jobs are significant contributors to this trend. The resulting unemployment and underemployment are the themes that stand out so starkly in the songs mentioned above.

Meanwhile, industry cannot find enough engineers, programmers, and people skilled in the trades. These high-demand positions do not have a correspondingly large labor pool to employ, so the pay and benefits increase to attract candidates, or the positions go unfilled.

Jadakiss, Naughty by Nature, and Kanye were lucky enough to have hit the jackpot, scoring the rare top-billing positions in Hip-Hop's highest tier of entertainers. Without that, their economic troubles would likely have carried on at least in part because of the cruel nature of the labor markets.

If the labor market and participation rates tell us about how many people are working, the Consumer Confidence Index (CCI) gives us an idea what those people are likely to do with their money: save it, spend it, or something else altogether . . . Since consumer spending is so important to the economy, market watchers follow the data like fat kids after an ice cream truck.

Business and government alike use the information to determine whether or not to proceed forward with product launches and costly capital expenditures. Downbeat results of the CCI tend to discourage quick and risky economic activity. Conversely, positive reports can send businesses on a veritable spending spree, making it rain with commercial commotion.

Hip-Hop music can serve as a type of consumer confidence index of its own. I know, right?! Mind blown. Sure, maybe it isn't a perfect corollary to the CCI survey of 5,000 American households and its formulaic analysis of current sentiments about the economy and expectations of future conditions as measured against the benchmark year of 1985. But the titles and lyrics of hit songs in Hip-Hop have tracked the trends of CCI.

When the U.S. economy was on fire in 1999, with some of the CCI's highest confidence figures, the Hip-Hop and R&B Top 40 reflected that optimism. Case's "Happily Ever After" talks about years of uninterrupted bliss. Ja Rule's "Holla Holla" had typically celebratory bluster about easy money and easy women. And there was the appropriately titled but crooning cheese-fest, "Fortunate," from Maxwell at #1.

If 1999 was the CCI's high watermark, 2009 was the low. You can see echoes of the recession in Cam'ron's song "I Hate My Job" with his comments about unpaid bills, rising costs, frustrations at work, and general pessimism. Lil Wayne's "Drop the World" expresses a fair bit of rage and frustration. Even the usually upbeat Flo Rida released "Rewind," calling back better days in the face of hard times.

Whether you choose to get your economic data from the sort of exciting sources like The Conference Board, Inc., the only 501(c)(3) tax-exempt non-profit business who can make teen girls swoon, with its super-sexy business membership and research work, or by listening to rappers tell it like it is on their tracks, consumer confidence is a useful tool for planning commercial pursuits.

If you've listened to more than one Rap song, you know all about the fun of having money. "Money, Cash, Hoes," "C.R.E.A.M.," "I Get Money," "Got Money," and the only slight variation on the theme "Got Your Money" are just the tip of the iceberg when it comes to Hip-Hop and its acquisitive obsession. The praise of monetary rewards might speak to the value of work for an entrepreneur. T.I., Jay-Z, and 50 Cent spit about spending cash in killer foreign locales that are meant to turn the listener green with envy. But what the lyrics of some pretty baller songs fail to reveal is how the value of that money actually works. Whether the artists knew it or not, the dollar's valuation heavily influences the big pimping, high-roller lifestyle of Hip-Hop.

You can do just about anything with the U.S. dollar. It became the world's most import currency after its victory in World War II. The United States' long-lasting economic power made its currency the go-to legal tender for international trade of essentials like agricultural products, steel, and oil sales. Even organized crime syndicates, terrorists, and rogue nations love their large-denomination dollars, as seen in the mountains of Benjamins seized in police raids or exchanged on the sly.

The value of the dollar (and most other currencies) is based on a few factors, and these are measured against one another in head-to-head matchups. There is the interest rate of a central bank or, in the case of the U.S., the Federal Reserve. There is a country's debt level, which for the U.S. is an eye-popping $18 trillion, and then there is the strength of its economy. When these indicators are strong (e.g., competitive interest rates, manageable debt, and a strong economy), the currency is strong and attractive. Conversely, when the opposite is true, a currency gets weaker relative to other nations' money.

The strength of a currency in international trade has a tremendous effect on a country's ability to import and export goods and services. When a currency is weak, the exchange rate allows someone with a stronger currency to buy more in the weaker economy. On the other hand, a strong currency makes exporting, service transactions, and even travel cost prohibitive or at least less attractive to people dealing in a weaker currency.

Sean "Jay-Z" Carter spent millions of dollars to make the iconic video "Big Pimpin" in Trinidad in 1999. When they filmed the video, the U.S. economy was doing big pimping of its own with dot coms blowing up stock exchanges, unemployment down to 4.1%, and government revenue surpluses. The exchange rate was 6.8 Trinidad and Tobago Dollars (TTD) to $1 US, which meant that Jay-Z's American bankroll went a long way in Trinidad and Tobago. But if the video had waited until the dark days of 2008, the world may have never seen Jay-Z, UGK, and the gorgeous Melyssa Ford cutting through the Caribbean in a super yacht. As the Great Recession began, the TTD/US exchange dropped to 5.9/$1 as a result of the collapse of the financial markets, unemployment rising to 7.3%, and U.S. debt reaching jaw-dropping heights. America's economic reversal would have essentially added 12% additional cost to "Big Pimpin" production expenses such as the rent of the yacht, payroll for the models, and local licenses and fees.

Maybe your business doesn't do any international trade, but understanding how dollar valuation and exchange works gives you an insight into factors affecting the wider economy. And even if you don't care about that, it is at least fun to think about rappers calculating their bar tabs in Euros on their next world tour . . .

Cycle of Scrilla: Cash at Work

Let's start at the top of the circle. For a business to begin operations, it needs money. It can either get that from a bank or the company leadership can use their own or some other investor's money. This seed money starts the wheel turning as it turns into overhead items like rent and utilities, labor, and the things that customers will ultimately buy.

As Rap music emerged as its own musical genre, Profile Records was there to launch artists and make Hip-Hop into a worldwide happening. However, Profile wouldn't have existed, and perhaps Hip-Hop's rise would have been delayed, if it hadn't been for the startup money that Cory Robbins and Steve Plotnicki decided to borrow to launch the label. In May of 1981, the two founders

Cash Cycle

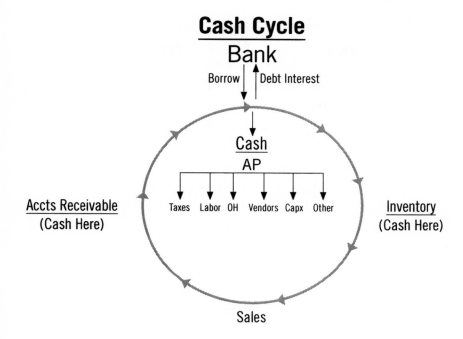

each borrowed $17,000 from their parents. "With the $34,000 in startup cash they rented a room for $700 a month in a building on the corner of Broadway and 57th Street."[3] Those offices, the utilities, supplies, and Robbins' and Plotnicki's professional drive at that stage in the company's development made possible the rise of Profile's biggest stars and grandfathers of Rap, Run-DMC.

Following the curve clockwise, that cash is employed to create the company's product, whatever that may be: software, crops, books, research for intellectual property, widgets, or Nicki Minaj-printed pillowcase covers. The creation of inventory sucks up cash with the hope that successful sales will turn it back into cash with more to show for it than existed previously.

When 50 Cent bought drugs from his suppliers, it was on consignment, which meant that he did not own the drugs free and clear at the time that they were given to him. He had to sell what he had in order to cover the cost of the raw materials and hopefully make a profit from a markup when he sold smaller retail quantities of crack.[4] Fortunately for 50 and his millions of fans, he was remarkably successful. Not Pablo Escobar or "El Chapo" Guzman successful, but successful enough to keep 50 from being murdered by angry and unforgiving suppliers. We'll take that as "good enough" in this case.

As we see at the bottom of the circle, the inventory or product goes out the door through sales to customers. Sales can take on nearly infinite variables in terms of product mix, volume, price, timing, and anything else that the seller or the customer might want. Without sales, the party stops as the cash cycle seizes up. Entrepreneurs know that without sales, nothing really matters, so they push hard to get them.

Snoop Dogg was a motivated salesman who wanted to take his product and turn it back into cash; and unlike some of his coworkers in the Long Beach branch of the Crips' Six One gang, Snoop was willing to do what it took to make a sale. According to him, "Most players on the street level . . . didn't like to sell anything less than a dub rock," which amounted to about $20, "but I was a hustler from jump, and I didn't mind breaking my ounces down to nickel and dime packages, or bumping them up to Five-O's or even half ounces. Whatever the traffic would bear." Snoop recognized that one salesperson's failure to satisfy a market demand made an opportunity for him. "My motto was always to give the customer what he wants and you'll never have to worry about the motherfuckers moving off somewhere else."[5] I couldn't have said it better myself. Thanks, Snoop.

The six o'clock to twelve o'clock positions of the cash cycle cover the period when cash returns to the business as part of Accounts Receivable, the accounting term for money owed to the company. Outside of direct retail sales, most payments are not made at the time of sale. Instead, payment terms offer a buyer timing flexibility to settle debts in 15-, 30-, 60-, 90-, or the dreaded 120-day periods. Once the cash is back in company hands, it is paid out in various directions:

- Back to the bank to cover debt and interest
- To the government in the form of taxes
- To employees in wages and bonuses
- To cover overhead, such as rent
- For utilities and insurance
- To vendors and suppliers supporting the company
- For capital expenditures that expand capacity
- Other

Profile Records was a good example of the beginning of the cash cycle, and it is also a good example of the return to the top of the circle. Plotnicki and Robbins were lucky to have found the Rap duo Dr. Jeckyll and Mr. Hyde. Their hit "Genius Rap" sold 150,000 12-inch singles. After costs for manufacturing, artists, and publishing royalties, the label founders still had about $150,000. "Although they didn't see all that money right away, they were both able to do two things within a few weeks: pay off their parents and start taking a salary."[6]

Profile expanded and created Hip-Hop's first music video to air on Music Television. (You have to remember that, once upon a time, MTV actually had videos . . .) With continued successes, namely Run-DMC, "Robbins and Plotnicki could afford to put some of it into marketing and promotion."[7]

Whether we are talking about Profile Records or any other business, the flow of money through the cycle is as essential to the survival of the business as blood pumping through the body. And just as with the human circulatory system, a severe enough blockage or breakdown in any part of it can lead to death. Understand the components of your cash cycle, and do what you have to do to keep it healthy.

Audio Accounting: Basic Bookkeeping

Rappers like Corey "C Murder" Miller, Radric "Gucci Mane" Davis, Amin "Rosco P. Coldchain" Porter, and Barry "Cassidy" Reese have all killed, but you might not have heard of Hip-Hop's most notorious hitman. His killing spree has spanned decades. He is remorseless and well-known. His victims include Sugar Hill Records, Ruthless Records, Luke Records, and Death Row Records. All of them were laid low by failures in accounting, and this killer remains at large today.

Accounting irregularities cost Death Row Records millions of dollars and high-quality artists at a time when it could ill afford it. Suge Knight played fast and loose with financial controls, and he was dead set against transparent accounting practices that he was afraid artists would use against him. Little did he realize that his failure to understand, let alone follow, Generally Accepted Accounting Practices would be a significant contributor to the demise of his label.

In briefs filed in court, Death Row's accounts were disorganized-by-design. "Death Row's accounts were always overdrawn, and their checks would have bounced in almost every case were it not for (Interscope, Death Row's distributor) accountants."[8]

Dr. Dre and Snoop Dogg both famously left Death Row with their pockets empty despite being at the high watermarks of their careers, owing to Suge's creative accounting. And despite his demigod status after his death, even Tupac Shakur couldn't get a fair shake from Death Row. According to the suit against Knight, Tupac had generated more than $60,000,000 in revenues for the label but somehow still owed Death Row $7,107,186.34 at the time of his death.[9] "Other artists, like Kurupt, of the Dogg Pound, were forced to file for bankruptcy a mere two years after his group's album went double platinum."[10] The devastating talent exodus, the $3 million settlement in favor of Tupac's estate and surrender of 150 master tapes are just a few of the catastrophes associated with poor accounting.

So what do you have to do in order to avoid the fate of failed Hip-Hop labels? We will cover a few accounting fundamentals to get you started, but smart money takes a lot more studying than what we cover here.

An accounting department records transactions, examines operational patterns, receives monies, and manages accounts payable, such as payroll and taxes. Accountants can monitor a business's strength, improve efficiencies, and use data to increase profitability when they are properly led. Oh, and they can keep you from going to jail for failure to comply with the laundry list of regulations. That is a pretty neat trick, too.

Reporting and compliance are the most important managerial functions of accounting. Reports are the interrelated tools that companies use to direct operations. Data from one report feeds information on the other reports, allowing managers to view operations and expenses from different perspectives. Good data will keep reports accurate, and bad data will flow from one report to another, corrupting the whole process. Regularly reviewing the financial data allows business leaders to recognize positive and negative trends and, under the best circumstances, make changes before it's too late. While there are more than a few accounting reports out there, some of the most popular are the balance sheet, cash flow statement, budgets, and income statements.

Bankers, owners, and people looking to buy a business love to see the balance sheet, since it says a lot about a company very quickly. The balance sheet is a snapshot, showing the condition of a company's assets, liabilities, and equity at a particular point in time. The assets include cash, accounts receivable, inventories, property, plant, and equipment. The liabilities incorporate accounts payable, debts, taxes, and accrued expenses (such as salaries and vacation). Equity involves capital, which is cash contributed for shares of stock, and retained earnings or the income left in the business after dividends are paid.

The cash flow statement shows how increases and decreases on the balance sheet and income influence cash. The elements on the statement can be analyzed individually to decide on operational and financial changes to improve the business. Cash flow is either positive and generating cash above expenses or negative and paying out more than it brings in. It can serve as a planning instrument to show the effects of increasing or decreasing sales, higher research and development expenses, or the toll of back taxes and fines. Leaders can use projections in cash flow to strengthen weak months with promotions, sales, or delaying capital expenditures.

Like the balance sheet and cash flow statement, the budget is another tool for decision-making. Budgets are estimates of earnings and expenses for a set period of time, and they serve as models that predict how the business will do given certain financial activities. Managers can use their estimates for sales over several months or a year to determine the best guess for revenue in a budgeting cycle. Similarly, expected costs can be computed to show what the company is likely to put out the door to employees and suppliers. When taken together, the budget can be an effective playbook for operations. They also make handy targets for employee performance when reviews are tied to reasonable budgets.

Just like Hip-Hop artists, the income statement has lots of names. There are the revenue statement, statement of financial performance, earnings statement, operating statement, profit and loss statement (or, for accountants who think they are pimps, the P&L). They all mean the same thing: it's a report that measures a company's financial performance over time. In the end, it shows either a profit or a loss. If you are the Vegas gambling type, we can add roulette's zeros for breakeven, too. The report is filled with all the same income and expense accounts as the budget, and a P&L can include the budget to make for quick comparisons of predictions to actual performance. If the budget is the target, the income statement is the report card for performance. Supervisors can and should adjust compensation based on the results.

There are generally two types of accounting: cash-basis and accrual accounting. Small businesses usually do cash-basis accounting, recording financial transactions when cash trades hands. Accrual-based accounting acknowledges that a company intends to pay a debt. But instead of deferring the income or expense until cash trades hands, accrual accounting records them at the time when the commitment is made, regardless of whether funds were transferred.[11]

Using the examples from the Cash Cycle, if 50 Cent and Snoop had made the extremely poor decision to faithfully record their drug deals with dope fiends and baseheads, they might have used cash-basis or accrual accounting. In cash-basis, 50 would have recorded his expenditures to pay back his suppliers in the month he gave them the money, not at the time he picked up the drugs. Conversely, if he had the bad idea to sell retail quantities of crack on credit, Snoop would have recorded the income from his sales at the time of his transaction and not when he received payment, which would have been never. Addicts are not considered to be remarkably creditworthy.

While they make great examples of the two types of accounting, 50 and Snoop were smart to set aside their bookkeeping obsessions and refrain from documenting transactions. Both of them probably would have done a lot longer prison terms if their first-rate accounting records for narcotics exchanges were swept up by the police at the time of their arrests. It is the exception that proves the rule that you need good accounting.

Cash Flo Rida: Break-Even Point

Everyone needs a goal to shoot for. In the early phases of a business, that marker is the break-even point. It is the position where the company's payments going out the door are equal to the money it brings in from the outside. Determining the break-even point requires a company to compile all of its expense (e.g., payroll, supplies, taxes, utilities, insurance, rent, etc.) to generate the zero point. This is the sales number based on the estimated price of a company's products or services required to equal the costs.

When business leaders look at the break-even point, they can decide how achievable the goal is. An ugly break-even point can drive managers to look for ways to lower costs, such as reducing headcount, eliminating supplies, lowering manufacturing expenses, or deferring maintenance. On the revenue side of the equation, the executives may look for ways to increase prices for products or services to more easily reach and exceed the break-even point to get to the profit side of the balancing point.

Steve Rifkind came from a family in entertainment. He parlayed his experience working with his dad into a gig promoting albums for small record labels in California (he called his company "SRC"). The business plan was to get music into circulation with the biggest splash possible. Rifkind and his team covered the four pathways of promotion of the time: retail, radio, video, and grass roots word-of-mouth tastemaking. He did it with a crew of "cool kids," for lack of a better term. The street team would call on record stores, Black radio stations, barbershops, gang hangouts, bars, and nightclubs to push the product that labels hired them to promote.[12]

Like everyone else in the industry, SRC had expenses and overhead to deal with, and the costs were not insignificant—somewhere between $45,000 and $60,000. There were printing costs for materials, an office in West Hollywood, payroll, telephone, and utilities. Although the street-promotion personnel weren't full-time employees, their performance-based retainers of $100 to $200 a week added up, given the size of the crew. To balance out the equation, SRC had to factor in its sales. The record labels paid Rifkind $15,000 to promote a music single. "If [SRC] could keep at least four clients at any one time, the business could make money."[13] That was the break-even point and the revenue line that the company had to clear to make a profit.

Rifkind was successful with SRC, and he would go on to start, operate, and sell several entertainment companies over the course of his career. He promoted Hip-Hop greats like the Akon, Big Pun, and the Wu-Tang Clan. Had he not known his break-even point back at the start of SRC days, he might have underpriced his services or overspent on operations, and the Hip-Hop community might have been shorted some of its most talented acts.

The Ball Street Journal: Moving Money

Businesses shuffle money in and out as part of operations, and we've seen some of that in the cash cycle. Cash flow is an accounting measurement that looks at the difference between the cash available at the beginning of a certain period of time and how much there is at the end of the accounting interval. The money available at the beginning is called the opening balance, and what there is at the end is the closing balance. If the closing balance is greater than the opening balance, you have positive cash flow. If there is less money at the end compared to the beginning, you have negative cash flow.

Cash flow helps leaders identify strengths and weaknesses in the operations. A company can improve the incoming cash with[14]

1. Increasing sales or raising prices
2. Getting money from the bank in the form of loans

3. Cutting costs
4. Paying vendors more slowly
5. Investing options

However, as a tool, cash flow has its limitations. Positive cash flow should not be confused with profit (I know, right?! You get used to it), and negative cash flow does not translate into a loss. There are accounting operations like the gradual depreciation of equipment, prepaid expenses like insurance premiums or rent, or customers who fail to pay their debts. These important categories aren't things that the company is pulling out of its bank accounts to cover, and so they don't affect the cash flow for the period. Cash flow has to be used in conjunction with the income statement or profit-and-loss report to get a sense of the health of a company which, ideally, will have positive cash flow and a profit.

Dana Elaine "Queen Latifah" Owens had a successful career as a rapper, pioneering roles for women in the genre, but she learned a hard lesson about cash flow. After her early successes with albums like *All Hail the Queen*, *Black Reign*, and *Order in the Court*, Latifah used her musical celebrity status to create new opportunities for herself in entertainment, including a production and talent-managing business called Flavor Unit Entertainment.

For a while, things at the new company were going well. Latifah was signing new artists and engaging in new projects. She was focused on the parts of the business she was comfortable with: event coordination, recording, album production, etc. Unfortunately, Latifah left the processing of payments and revenue collections to an accounting student with no practical experience and no oversight. In the spring of 2000, Flavor Unit went bankrupt.

> *Using the signature card I gave him, he [the accounting student] wrote check after check after check to pay off*

every bill that came into the office, not even question-
ing the amounts. Then, just as he was getting ready to
pay off another pile of invoices coming due, he noticed
something was off . . . 'I, uh . . . Okay, I'm just gonna
say it. There's no money left in your account.'[15]

The bookkeeper had put $500,000 out the door in a matter of just a few months. For a small business, 500 G's was a ton of cash . . . obviously more than the company was making. Latifah was stunned, but things got worse. She had scheduled payments of $1 million due to the IRS, and there was no money to cover the taxes. How could she be making as much money as she was making and still have run out of money? The answer was that Latifah had not gone to the trouble to examine Flavor Unit's cash flow to see what effect operations were having, positive or negative.

Latifah was able to right the ship at the company, but it was painful. She had to lay off much of her workforce, and she arranged a payment plan with the IRS to cover her tax obliga-tions. But none of that would have been necessary if she had only understood and monitored her company's cash flow. And Latifah's troubles make an excellent entrée into our next subject.

Intaxication: Business and Government Obligations

People have been paying for government going back to the beginning of the division of labor in ancient societies. The tradi-tion of paying for some kind of societal administration continued on to present times; and in the US today, the Internal Revenue Service, better known by its totally sick acronym, IRS, is respon-sible for the collection of taxes. Just as a business needs cash to function, so, too, does the federal government. Oh, and by the way, so do state and local governments, too. Expect them to have their hands out, looking for their share of the tax obligations every business has.

Taxes come in all shapes and sizes. How a business is con-
stituted, whether a corporation, limited liability company, sole
proprietorship, or partnership drives the kinds of taxes due and
the way in which they are paid.

Federal income tax is a pay-as-you-go tax, meaning a company
pays the tax as it earns income throughout the year. There are
two ways to pay as you go: withholding and estimated taxes.
Most people are familiar with withholding taxes. They are the
ones that disappear out of your paycheck before it ever gets to
you because your employer forwards them on to the government.
Uncle Sam likes to get paid first.

Estimated taxes cover income that is not subject to withholding, such as income from self-employment, interest, dividends,
prizes, and awards.[16] The taxes are figured off of a company's
income in the past as well as projected income for the coming
year. Similar to withholding taxes taken each pay period, the
government likes to get its estimated tax payments regularly,
so they are generally made in four equal payments throughout
the year.

Queen Latifah had a run-in with the IRS when her company,
Flavor Unit, ran out of money. They had paid out too much too
quickly to vendors without reserving enough funds for their tax
obligations. The whole situation was a shock to Latifah and
the kind of stress that turns hair gray quickly. Fortunately, the
Internal Revenue Service generally isn't out to pick a fight when
it doesn't have to. The law allows the IRS to waive penalties for
underpayment when there is a casualty event, disaster, or other
unusual circumstance. And this was the reasoning that Latifah
and Flavor Unit's accountants used when explaining their circumstance to the IRS. They made a case to the effect that, "Hey,
we made a huge mistake what with using a college kid as the
corporate bookkeeper. We had poor supervision and oversight
of our accounting function. But we know we screwed up, and

we are going to make things right." It was enough to satisfy the taxman, and it gave Flavor Unit a chance to recover.

Taxes are serious business, and they can be super complicated. When in doubt, get professional help to understand your obligations. And when all else fails, have a good story to tell the auditors and plan to fix the problems.

99 PROBLEMS: HIGH-LEVEL MANAGEMENT AND MAJOR CHANGES IN BUSINESS

T HE ONLY THING THAT STAYS the same is change, and businesses have to be able to adapt to survive. At its height in the 1990s, Death Row Records had more than $100 million in annual revenue, and it was revered in the Hip-Hop community. Suge Knight had money, power, and prestige like almost no other in Rap music up to that point in time. However, years later, as Suge returned to jail following charges of vehicular assault and homicide of two associates in 2015, he probably wondered how it could all have gone so wrong. The answer was, of course, his own inability to deal with the changes that life in business inevitably bring.

When the end came for Suge Knight and Death Row Records, it really shouldn't have been a surprise. He had let down his artists with shady accounting and delayed album releases. He drove off or lost his best talent by promoting a brutal and autocratic culture at the label. Suge failed to diversify his artistic lineup even as Hip-Hop tastes started to change. He couldn't tolerate competing ideas, so he never mentored new leaders or delegated meaningful responsibilities. In addition, if all of that weren't bad enough, Suge couldn't control himself enough to avoid the violent conflicts that ultimately landed him in prison.

Business leaders need to prepare themselves, their people, and organizations for changes. Some of them might be desirable, such as corporate sales, mergers, and acquisitions. Others are unpredictable and inescapable. By reviewing leadership's most challenging events, managers can arm themselves to face them with more information, greater confidence, and a better chance of success.

Go Big or Go Home: Commercial Risk-Taking

Senior leaders have to take chances to protect or grow the business. Ford spun the roulette wheel with the mass production of his Model T and changed the face of manufacturing and the world. In 1995, Mitchell Energy's gamble bought themselves a new lease on life in the oil business and revolutionized energy markets with the creation of hydraulic fracturing mineral extraction. Amazon pushed all its chips into the center of the table with online shopping, and retailers around the world are feeling the reverberations of their roll of the dice. Uncertain ventures are vital to the creative process; they keep companies relevant in the marketplace since they can generate outsized benefits for the company and its people. Organizations that take risks stand out from the competition for the *cojones* they display trying something new, sometimes even on projects that don't pan out . . .

Executives can use planning processes, directed innovation, and risk-management structures to lay the groundwork for smart risk-taking. We've already talked about parts of those topics earlier, and they remain relevant here. Planning needs the resource lists of required people and assets. Innovation efforts require a willingness to listen to team members, suppliers, and customers, as well as the acceptance of failures. Risk management also includes a catalog of factors affecting a job. Still, good, calculated commercial risks require a bit more work to improve the chances for success. Senior managers have to organize for the endeavor, get buy-in from people who matter, and forge ahead through the difficulties that are an inevitable part of risk-taking.

Anyone who has to organize activities in a business gamble had better bring their A game. Taking the organization out on a limb can get the juices flowing from the YOLO way of doing business. After the team has come up with the genius ideas that are going to revolutionize the industry, leadership needs to evaluate the program to see if it is worth the trouble. The less difficult and resource intensive a risk is, the easier it is to get approved. Think of cosmetic changes like alternative colors in a manufactured product, simple coding improvements to software functionality, or robbing a slightly different kind of high-end retailer.

As risk proposals increase in complexity, the need to analyze and explain the plan grows, too. The idea of firing a long-time customer to free up resources in favor of more profitable sales elsewhere should identify target customers who can plug the revenue gap created, and it should detail the likelihood of closing the new deals. Financial service providers who propose to increase their lending have to explain how to cover capital-on-hand requirements for regulating bodies, and they must show why the institutions getting the money are going to be able to pay back the larger debt loads. The intent is to classify the change in operations as an acceptable risk that can be managed. As part of the analysis for the risk proposal, managers should create goals they expect to meet with the change. Sales will increase in this demographic by X percent. Scrap and reject rates will decrease by Y with this material substitution. Or this calculated wardrobe malfunction during the Grammies on a female star will generate an increase of Z online hits. To the extent it is possible, managers should carry out testing, focus groups, and modeling to support assumptions. Being able to articulate the plan and its hazards is very valuable, but as Russell Simmons found out, it isn't the only problem with risk-taking.

Anyone who's ever seen Simmons knows he takes great pride in his appearance and, especially, his clothes. It was no surprise that he had the vision to create a successful, Black-owned clothing line with Phat Farm. He thought, "Why should African-American entertainers and Hip-Hop fans boost the sales of White-owned fashion lines when they weren't all that reflective of the tastes of the community?" Phat Farm would use high-quality materials and manufacturing. The clothes would be slightly oversized to meet the Hip-Hop style of the time, and Phat Farm would carry the motto "Classic American Flava." Simmons's goal was to build a brand that people could buy in upscale national retailers, namely Macy's and Bloomingdale's.

Simmons had his plans. He'd picked out the store location. He knew the materials he wanted for the clothes. He knew who would do his design work and manufacturing. He even knew how much it was going to cost . . . and it cost a lot. What he didn't know because he hadn't done very extensive market research was which products would be popular and which ones would just collect dust on store shelves. Phat Farm paid a fortune for clothing designs that no one bought. "For every item that Phat Farm sold, there were more that didn't."[1] Simmons spoke plainly about his financial exposure resulting from the risks he took with the brand, saying, "I lost money for six straight years, to the tune of $10 million. Not someone else's money—my money."[2]

The costs of the operation and its trajectory were enough to make one of Phat Farm's investors squeamish and forced Simmons to buy him out, leaving Simmons to pour more of his own money into the venture. Fortunately for him (and for people who love argyle sweaters), Simmons was able to weather the storm and make corrections to the business plan. Phat Farm would be a significant fashion presence with the Hip-Hop community throughout the 1990s. Although, with a little more effort examining his risks and assessing the market, Simmons might have avoided some of the early missteps, the important lesson is that he found a business idea worth trying. Simmons deserves mad props for putting himself and his money out there. Because that's what ballers do.

Organizing for the business gamble makes it easier for the politicking, salesmanship, and stakeholder management to get buy-in. Getting some kind of acceptance from others for risks helps ensure that a proposal gets the time, money, and resources it needs to succeed. The riskier the program, the more important it is to have people informed and on board with the activities that have so much riding on them. Also, if things go badly, buy-in reduces a manager's risk of being set adrift by leaders looking for a scapegoat. After all, misery loves company, and teamwork means never having to take all of the blame yourself.

In the stakeholder management of project management, teams put together categorized lists of people who could affect or have interest in an endeavor. Senior leaders looking to roll the dice will need that list to push the business plan. Knowing who has power and motivation in the organization to help or hurt the plan will drive the buy-in effort. The more power a stakeholder has, the more work is required to win them over. Even though the business plan may be carefully crafted after the initial organizing, there is an advantage to opening it up for criticism when talking to key people. Allowing others to analyze the proposal provides leaders the opportunity to correct weaknesses and demonstrates to supporters and naysayers alike that their input matters. It might be trite, but using "we" in the course of the sales pitch can have subtle effects to include the audience emotionally. Even if the whole company is on board with a risk proposal, there is no guarantee they will remain that way. Keeping people in the loop on how the program is going is a good way to maintain support. An informed audience is a more predictable audience.

People who drove Jeeps loved them enough to get their own nickname, Jeepers. They waved to one another on the road. They'd occasionally take them off-road to challenge their four-wheel drive. And best of all for Chrysler, they spent bigly to soup up their rides . . . or just to keep them running. Unfortunately for the automaker, the company had a very hard time trying to figure out how to create more Jeepers to buy the vehicles. In the first few years of the new century, sales for the iconic Wrangler and Grand Cherokee declined by as much as 25 percent at a time when auto and light-truck sales nationwide were generally steady. Something needed to change.

Marques McCammon worked for an automotive innovation firm called American Specialty Cars, and he believed that he could help Chrysler skew its demographics younger and capture a larger market share by leveraging Jay-Z's name on a tricked-out version of the Jeep Commander. SUV sales more than doubled for Ford in the early 1990s when they associated the designer Eddie Bauer's name with their Explorer model. McCammon argued that Jay-Z's star power could have the same effect for Jeep's slumping sales in 2004. With a little effort, he had consent from Jay-Z to proceed. McCammon had his risk proposal. The vehicle would be a relatively high-end SUV retailing for about $50,000, with a deluxe sound system, 22-inch chrome wheels, and signature Jay-Z Blue. The plan was to create an initial run of 1,000 Jay-Z Jeep Commanders, with more to follow when sales picked up.

McCammon just needed the buy-in to make his idea a reality. He took his plan and shopped it around the automaker. "I probably went to four different executive-level meetings with directors and VPs inside of marketing at Chrysler."[3] According to McCammon, Chrysler executives were on board with the "cross-promotional vehicle," but in the week before Jay-Z would fly to

Detroit to ink the deal, Chrysler management backed out. It isn't clear that McCammon's plan for the Jay-Z Jeep was convincing. Where were the historical examples of comparable vehicle sales? What was the marketing plan for dealerships after the Jay-Z red-carpet debut was over? How was the Jay-Z Commander at its price point going to attract enough people in the target demographic to turn a profit? The buy-in just wasn't there.

Chrysler would continue to muddle along as the weak sister of the Big Three automakers, leading the crowd into bankruptcy in 2009. Nothing McCammon could have done would have prevented that. But who knows? If he had been more successful getting buy-in with a stronger marketing plan to make executives more comfortable with the risk, the Jay-Z Jeep might have been a game changer.

Once the risk proposals are complete and key players have bought in, the team needs to forge ahead. The best plans don't do anything until someone puts them in action, and that is when business leaders really need to lead. The risks to the company in the event of failure still exist whether they are minor inconveniences on the Profit and Loss Statement that can be brushed off all the way up to "game over" events ending the enterprise. Taking that seriously is an important part of driving to success.

Attitude is a huge determining factor for success. Positivity can have the constructive effect of creating a self-fulfilling prophecy, and, on risky ventures, every little bit helps to meet goals. Especially when making a commercial roll of the dice, things aren't always going to go right, but leaders who recognize and correct problems increase people's confidence. It shows honesty and a will to succeed, which people love. Companies can refund or replace defective product. Law firms that make errors with new legal processes can meet with clients to assess damages and find remedies. And dealers dabbling in new dope can take feedback from the fiends on the quality of their Phenazepam and switch suppliers.

When they come along, bosses should celebrate the successes of the program. Taking the time to observe little victories reminds team members, customers, and suppliers that things are going in the right direction, and that keeps people optimistic about the prospects of the risk proposal. The fêtes for the crew can be modest, like getting pizza for shipping orders on time, or wild, like making it rain at a strip club for landing a new anchor account. Even if the corporate staff doesn't appreciate the latter revels, the strippers will.

The last point in staying positive on high-risk missions is the need to stamp out negativity. It is one thing to point out difficulties; leadership should address problems quickly after identification. It is another thing for team members to dog the program with steady criticism or a can't-do attitude. If positivity can create profitable self-fulfilling prophecies, negativity can do the same thing in the opposite direction. Using information and emotion to combat pessimism usually works. Communicating how the team addresses challenges and highlighting the victories won is a good start. If the bad vibes are coming from suppliers or even team members, executives may need to discuss an attitude adjustment or do a little "addition by subtraction," cutting them loose if the naysayers don't get in line after a sit-down.

Queen Latifah was lucky to have the parents she did, since they managed the uncertain task of raising kids like pros. The thing that came through most clearly in all of her stories of growing up was her mother's and father's commitment to a positive outcome for their children. Things weren't easy for Rita and Lancelot Owens, Queen Latifah's parents. Rather than raising their kids in Newark, New Jersey, where it would be difficult to escape the depression of that city's steady decline, they moved to better neighborhoods in surrounding areas.

They did everything they could to set their children up for success. Latifah's mother organized field trips to museums and the zoo to expand their horizons. Her father took her camping in the rain to teach her that life wasn't always going to be easy. Both of them insisted on their kids attending church and Catholic schools to reinforce the moral values that they pushed. Even when Latifah's parents got divorced, Rita and Lancelot tried to make arrangements that were not disruptive to their children's lives. In her own words, her parents' positivity was effective.

> *Sometimes all it takes is a word to instill self-confidence and self-esteem in someone. For me, it was my parents telling me I could do anything . . . the more you try, the more surface area you create in which to succeed. And from success, you gain self-confidence.*[4]

Latifah would go on to record seven studio albums, at least three of which went gold. She was nominated for dozens of awards for film and music, winning more than twenty. She supported a number of social movements and charities. Those are pretty good measures of success, and Latifah draws a straight line from her victories back to Rita and Lancelot and their attitudes in the risky business of parenting.

Lawyer Up: Legal Concerns

Dating from 1754 BC, the Code of Hammurabi had some of the first written laws dealing with business; and since the time of that simple list of 200-odd rules, things have only gotten more complicated. Well-intentioned civic leaders passed regulations aimed at funding government, advancing trade, and preventing kids from being ground into hamburger. But why stop there? The Federal Register, the repository for laws in the US, has grown to almost 80,000 pages of rules, regulations, and codes that direct nearly every aspect of life. And just in case there was something the feds missed, state and local governments have their own laws regulating businesses, such as the Massachusetts law requiring children to brush their teeth at daycare, the Philadelphia license required for blogging, or even Milwaukee's going-out-of-business license. The volume and complexity of regulation ensures that no team, let alone individual entrepreneur, can navigate the hazardous waters of business law without expert advice.

Knowing when to ask for outside help is just smart business. Capable lawyers can provide the education in unfamiliar areas that entrepreneurs and executives need to make their visions into reality and limit the damage inflicted when things go wrong. Effective legal advice can smooth planning processes, protect company interests, and keep the company in the good graces of the government. Executives can find their team through personal referrals, industry-association recommendations, or plain old Google searches using the specific legal topics in the search field. Similar to any other supplier or contractor, managers should vet their lawyers for relevant experience, good communications, and reasonable fees.

Getting legal support specific to the business's industry in planning activities can reduce downside effects significantly. In the early phases of a business, lawyers can provide expert advice on incorporating a company, counseling on required permits and licenses for operations, and guidance on how the industry works. Entrepreneurs can use their legal team to explain Fair Practice, covering fun topics like energy colossus Enron-style price fixing, agribusiness giant ADM-inspired conspiracy to allocate markets, or old-timey Standard Oil illegal monopolies. There are plenty of other business-planning subjects worth reviewing with the lawyers. For example, Privacy Law is gaining in importance because it covers things such as the protection of consumer data, child-privacy rights online, and company responsibilities in the event of data breaches. Advice on Advertising and Marketing Law can keep companies on safe ground relating to truth-in-advertising, marketing claims, and e-mail spam.

Good lawyers can save the day by alerting management to statutory pitfalls before anyone stumbles into them. It is up to team members to incorporate the lessons from their expensive legal assistance into checklists and plans. Where appropriate, managers should create guidance based on counsel for wider dissemination within the organization. Eventually, as team members get more familiar with the law, the company can reduce its dependence on outside legal support reducing costs. Instead, the business can employ lawyers for specialized functions or complex tasks that occur less frequently.

History is replete with the torture-porn type tragedies of artists getting screwed out of their fair share of the loot they create. Hip-Hop has plenty of examples of it with Soulja Boy, Ma$e, and KRS-One being just a few of them. The pattern of abuse is actually understandable. In most cases, the bad deals resulted from the artists' inexperience and poor understanding of the agreements put in front of them. There was rarely good legal representation at the artist's side to explain the inner workings of the music industry, provide instruction on the fine print, and do it all for reasonable fees.

L.A. lawyer Julian Petty grew up with Hip-Hop in Long Island. The 1980s Rap star Rakim regularly rode around the neighborhood in plain sight. Dave of the group De La Soul would give Petty haircuts as a kid. The future lawyer even got Rap lessons from Professor Griff of Public Enemy to make a demo tape. Those gave him good *bona fides* as he finished college and started work in the industry.

Petty didn't much care for the ugly pattern of financial abuse that he saw for artists. Inspired by another Hip-Hop attorney icon, L. Londell McMillan, he decided that he would be the lawyer that artists could turn to for honest counsel. As a partner at Nixon Peabody, LLP, he represents rappers like Earl Sweatshirt (performer of "Hive" and "Chum"), Freddie Gibbs (famous for

"BFK" and "Fuckin Up the Count"), and Vince Staples (best known for "Prima Dona" and "Norf Norf").

"[Petty] completely understands the background of his artists," Staples says. "There's a deeper bond between him and the craft than most lawyers because he's passionate about and understands the importance of quality and legacy."[5]

Representing a number of big-name clients or their estates, Petty made sure that the people who hired him comprehended the activity going on. He worked with Earl Sweatshirt to understand the complexities of a publishing and merchandise deal with Sony. He represented the estate of Christopher "Notorious B.I.G." Wallace for the use of the artist's lyrics in the *Notorious* movie as well as worked to get Biggie-branded clothes into stores. The money that clients earn . . . or keep . . . depends in no small part on the early education that Julian Petty and lawyers like him provide. If it works for them, then professionals in business would do well to figure in legal aid early in planning.

Good legal coverage continues past early education and initial planning concerns onto activities to protect company interests. Any business has something worth protecting: trade secrets, patents, copyrights, sales agreements, arrangements with suppliers, or financial assets like stocks, debts, or other rights and privileges. These make up the special sauce of the commercial enterprise, and work would at least be harder, if not impossible, without them. When properly employed, lawyers can be there to manage intellectual property to maintain control of great ideas. They can help companies structure bulletproof financial contracts with customers and suppliers. The legal team can make sure that arrangements with equity, debt, and other fiscal transactions give stakeholders their due—something that is especially important in highly regulated industries. In dark times, such as during litigation or lawsuits, a company's attorney can fight for its rights in court or recommend a settlement to keep the costs of justice in line with the benefit.

Employees may know some things about intellectual property, contracts, or finance law, and they should do their jobs without hesitation on predictable business. However, it is time to call in the big guns when things start to get complicated or the real or potential dollar value of deals starts to climb. An attorney's review of contracts and agreements should be like the goalie, the last line of defense before finalizing a deal. There isn't much upside to saving a few hundred or thousand dollars in legal fees if corporate officers sign off on agreements that hurt the business . . . sometimes to the tune of hundreds of thousands or millions of dollars.

The law and the entertainment industry have been close ever since there were big fortunes to be made . . . and lost. It is a relationship that already goes back several generations now. Lawyers played pivotal roles in Hip-Hop almost since the start of the genre, mostly for standard stuff like artist contracts, the buying, selling, and liquidation of record labels, and occasionally trying to clear performers of drugs, weapons, and murder charges. All of these jobs played their part in protecting the interests of the various stakeholders involved. Frankly, from its start through to the mid-1990s, there wasn't much new to any of the legal work. The explosion of the Internet changed all of that.

Record sales began a precipitous and prolonged drop as fans found, downloaded, and listened to the music they loved for free. File sharing was terrifying for labels and artists alike because both groups were losing money every day that the piracy went on. Bootlegging music was nothing new, but no one had ever seen it on the scale found on popular sites like Napster. Some feared that the uncontrolled abuse of artists' work and intellectual property would signal the end of the music industry.

The godfather of Gangsta Rap, Dr. Dre, knew about intellectual property rights. He had sworn off sampling other artists' music on the tracks he produced when he started Aftermath Entertainment, just to stay clear of the muddy waters of fair usage and royalty payments. Dre knew the costs associated with legally incorporating others' work, and it wasn't worth it to him. Dre wanted that money for himself and his artists, so it made perfect sense that he wasn't going to take the hit to his income lying down when it came to the kingpin of file sharing. He decided to get legal on Napster's ass.

Dre and others teamed up to hire Howard King, the L.A. lawyer of King, Holmes, Paterno & Soriano, LLP. Standing on solid legal ground, King said:

> We wrote a letter [Monday] on behalf of Dr. Dre to Napster basically putting them on notice that the listing of his songs and masters on Napster and the facilitation of the transfer of those files constitutes an infringement of his copyrights.[6]

Other heavyweights like RIAA, record labels, and even the Heavy Metal band Metallica joined the fight against file-sharing companies. The combined forces of the music industry and years of legal wrangling shut down Napster's services until the file-sharing company was able to provide compensation to Dre for his work and assurances that they would control the piracy occurring on its site. Without the aid of competent legal support, it is hard to say where Dre or anyone in entertainment would be right now.

As an added bonus, the parties settled the case out of court, saving everyone a chunk of change. That was probably helpful since Napster had to make an initial payout of $26 million to Dre and the others. Justice costs a lot, so it frequently pays to seek mediation, arbitration, and/or settlements in favor of full court cases.

A company still has legal compliance to consider even after education, planning, and interest-protecting actions. The government has things it expects businesses to do, and management teams need to find ways to meet those expectations. Once again, legal support is there to help organizations comply with employment and labor law, environmental regulations, and workplace health and safety rules.

Modern businesses can thank the cruelty, exploitation, and mismanagement of nineteenth- and early twentieth-century employers (with a little help from recent examples of corporate malfeasance) for the multifarious labor-law environment they experience today. Yes, apparently all you needed to do was carry out arbitrary mass firings, withhold earned wages, and blatantly discriminate against all kinds of people for years on end to bring down the thunder of the government, with thousands of pages of rules on do's and don'ts of employee management. There are tangles of requirements for overtime pay calculations, equal employment opportunity, and/or accommodations for legal marijuana usage. While good human resource employees can go a long way toward keeping a company straight, a little legal backup can make sure that things remain aboveboard for items such as non-compete agreements, reduction in wages, and disability accommodations.

Environmental, health, and safety regulations bring their own compliance challenges. Again, these rules are in place thanks to gross abuse in the past, such as the 10 million gallons of oil spilled by the Exxon Valdez in 1989, the dozens of women with radiation sickness resulting from their work for the United States Radium Corporation in 1917, or the 1911 Triangle Shirtwaist Factory fire that killed 146 workers. Although most companies don't pour oil into the ocean, make their employees glow in the dark, or lock workers in sweatshops without means of escape, there are plenty of smaller government regulations that add to the difficulty of compliance. Labor and environmental lawyers can counsel companies about government changes to rules, review corporate policies, and provide examples of industry best practices. This can keep businesses compliant with the law and still capable of turning a profit.

When Jay-Z got involved with Tidal, the subscription-based music-streaming service, he liked its progressive politics. It provided the "highest percentage of royalties to music artists and songwriters" of comparable companies and was artist owned.[7] It was a means to get out a message . . . oh, and Jay-Z could make a crap-ton of money with high-quality streaming. That counted, too. However, Tidal's connection to Hip-Hop royalty and progressive politics did not exempt it from observance of employment law.

Lisette Paulson was an artist-relations consultant for Tidal, and she made it into the news when she sued her company for a laundry list of violations, including:

> . . . *sex and pregnancy discrimination, intentional infliction of emotional distress, breach of oral contract and violation of the New York Civil Rights Act, Patient Protection and Affordable Care Act, Fair Labor Standards Act and New York State Labor Law.*[8]

Paulson alleged that, following her return from a medical leave of absence to have a child, Tidal executives denied her the use of a private space to pump breast milk, and she was fired shortly thereafter for her trouble.

Jay-Z's wife, Beyoncé's, burn album, *Lemonade*, showed the world that he was in hot water over another woman's breasts, and with his less-than-secret extramarital affairs, he might have seen that relationship trouble coming. Jay-Z probably didn't expect his financial interests at Tidal to get burned over a different set of breasts . . . in this case, Lisette Paulson's. It just goes to show that knotty issues like employment law can haunt companies whose staff is uninformed and unprepared.

Empire State of Mind: Mergers and Acquisitions (M&A)

Businesses are there to provide value to the customers and make money. In order to achieve one or both of those things, enterprises will buy or merge with other companies in the belief that M&A helps achieve growth. Combining the resources of two companies can create synergies that neither organization had separately. Wealthy but sleepy corporations may acquire cash-strapped-but-expanding startup operations using the corporation's dough to finance the startup's fast growth. Companies can increase their scale through M&A to improve purchasing power for supplies, raw materials, and utilities, or they can eliminate redundant work done by both businesses, increasing profits.

M&A also allows firms to diversify their product offerings. For example, Walt Disney Company leads the parks and recreation market with iconic Disneyland sites around the globe. Other divisions focus on consumer products and interactive media, making and retailing toys. Rounding out the package for Disney are the media networks like ESPN, A+E Networks, and ABC. Together, they represent an entertainment goliath. In a different twist on M&A, organizations can double-down in their market, such as brewing giant InBev, with its assembly of 200 beer brands, including heavy hitters like Corona, Budweiser, and Stella Artois. If you want name-brand beer, the chances are you're drinking an InBev product. In still another strategy, companies can grow with vertical integration by acquiring suppliers and distribution channels, as Apple did by combining a myriad of functions under one corporate umbrella. The company designs hardware for iPads, iPhones, and Macs. It creates its own software and apps, and it manages services like iTunes. It even retails most of its products out of the Apple Store. From product manufacture to retail and ending with in-app purchases, Apple gets a piece of the profit every step of the way.

Every M&A transaction is unique, but business leaders can evaluate deals with some common considerations. Acquisitions need to resolve concerns about the consolidation of the two companies. The buyers need to have a vision for what the purchased operation will do, and they need to make it happen once the deal is done. Purchasers are responsible for due diligence, a process that looks at every part of the new business and deciding how it will fold into the new, larger enterprise. Due diligence may show that an acquisition target is a bad deal, shutting it down before it goes anywhere. Accounting, computer systems, personnel, inventory, equipment, facilities, purchasing functions, products, sales force, and everything else need evaluation and strategies for incorporation. The buyer should save value-added departments and reduce or eliminate unnecessary expenses.

In the 1980s, there were six major record labels: Warner Music, CBS, Polygram, EMI, RCA, and MCA. Although there were fewer labels than in previous decades, there were still supply-side options for artists. They could still sign with any of the major labels or independent record companies. On the demand side, there were plenty of places for labels to sell product: record stores, radio stations, and fledgling, music-oriented music media outlets like MTV. For the most part, people in the industry could rely on certain power dynamics based on the labels' ability to control distribution. At the time, record companies held most of the cards.

The Internet changed that. File sharing, Internet music purchases, and live streaming had a devastating effect on record companies' sales. The power dynamic of musical distribution had shifted significantly. The labels had to negotiate across a wide network for distribution of their product just to stay relevant. Digital revenues were the fastest-growing segment of the industry, so the majors needed to figure out how to get back in control. Part of that desire for control meant that the industry would consolidate from six major labels down to four and from four to three . . .

In 2011, Universal Music Group and Sony decided that being bigger would give them more leverage over distribution through digital music service providers. The two companies would buy portions of London-based E M I, the old home of classic Hip-Hop acts like the Geto Boys, Raekwon, and Master P. Universal would get E M I's recorded music operations for $1.9 billion. Sony got part of E M I's music publishing division for some portion of $2.2 billion. Sony and Universal were more formidable with the best assets of E M I divided between them, and as anticipated, both companies were able to negotiate better agreements with their distributors. Unfortunately for industry competition, there were now only three major labels: Universal, Sony, and Warner.

Just as every other part of a good business comes with a plan, acquisitions need to be thought out. Every purchase agreement should have a set price and select how the acquiring company will pay for it. The options available to arrange a purchase are so numerous and complex that companies need professional help prior to any deal. There is the classic way to pay—with straight cash, which is usually attractive to sellers looking for their big payday. However, that can be costly if the purchasing company cannot get a good deal to borrow money for the acquisition because of interest rates or a bank's demands when loaning funds. After all, banks want their payday, too . . .

The acquiring company can offer stock in the organization, giving equity or partial ownership to the people selling out. This route can be tricky since offering stock or partial ownership also grants a certain amount of power and influence over the business. There is seller financing, which uses cash generated from the operations of the newly purchased company to pay its owners back over time. This cash-flow-financing arrangement puts more risk on the selling team, since deals occasionally fail to deliver the intended value, and delayed payouts may never arrive. There are ways to structure deals to provide protections to buyers and sellers like indemnifications, insurance, holdback arrangements, and escrow, which is essentially placing securities in the custody of a third party for a time when conditions of the sale have been fulfilled. Buyers can incentivize reluctant sellers with earn-out provisions providing future payments if the combined operation does better than expected. Earn-outs are complicated enough so that companies considering them should make sure that the agreement is watertight to avoid litigation.

With just about 60 million subscribers, Sprint Corporation was in a distant fourth place in the US wireless carrier industry. That put it behind Verizon, AT&T, and even scrappy T-Mobile. Because consumers viewed wireless services as an interchangeable commodity, Sprint's leadership wanted to find a way to differentiate itself from its competition to gain market share, so it looked to Jay-Z's Tidal streaming music to give it an edge.

Jay-Z bought Tidal for $56 million in 2015, and his star power, exclusive musical releases, and the brand's progressive pay structure for artists kept the business in the news. That was enough to get Sprint to offer $200 million for a 33 percent stake in the business. As an extra incentive to make the deal, Jay-Z and his team would remain in place to run the company; but Sprint's CEO, Marcelo Claure, would join Tidal's board of directors to ensure that Sprint's interests were represented in business decisions. In all likelihood, Jay-Z added a buy-sell agreement to the deal that spelled out the terms for unloading the remainder of his interests in Tidal to Sprint at a future date. The real question would be whether Tidal and perhaps even Sprint would be around when the time came.

Tidal was the runt of the streaming music industry in the US. It had only 3 million paying subscribers, compared with Spotify's

40 million and Apple's 20 million.[9] Even after years in business and despite $2.1 billion in revenue, Tidal failed to turn a profit. Sprint, too, was in an unenviable position with losses of more than $400 million in 2016 on top of another $800 million lost in 2015. Although they considered Tidal an inexpensive entrée into the market, the wireless carrier's streaming-service-acquisition gamble was no sure way to turn around a tough situation for its primary business.

Mergers and acquisitions carry with them a laundry list of issues related to liabilities, taxes, and transaction fees. During due diligence, a purchasing company may learn that the target firm is in distress due to environmental, legal, or financial challenges. Where a full sale may transfer those liabilities to the buying organization, a straight asset sale (purchasing only the equipment, vehicles, inventories, and/or facilities) can shed some or all liabilities, leaving them with the former owners. Acquisitions may be taxable, and the purchaser needs to understand tax rates as part of the deal. The parties can structure some transactions in a tax-deferred manner, reducing immediate costs. Again, tax planning will require expert advice. Sales come with legal, broker, and accounting fees at a minimum, and buyers and sellers will need to negotiate who pays for what as part of the agreement.

Depending on the ownership arrangement, how big companies are in their industries, or what kinds of regulations exist, companies may need to seek approvals to conduct a sale. Boards of directors, stockholders, lenders, or government agencies like the Securities and Exchange Commission, Department of Justice, Federal Communications Commission, and/or Federal Trade Commission may need to sign off on sales. Each approval authority will have its own requirements that buyers and sellers will need to meet prior to getting the green light for closing. Boards and stockholders want to make sure that they are getting properly compensated for selling the company. Lenders need to be sure that they get paid the money they are owed, and government agencies want to be sure that consolidating companies will not negatively impact consumers, prices, or fair trade by limiting competition or creating illegal monopolies.

Universal's initial proposal to purchase EMI came with significant regulatory scrutiny in Europe. The music behemoth wanted the record label because of its control of valuable music catalogs and the bargaining power it would have to negotiate highly profitable rates with streaming services and other demand-side revenue outlets. The European Commission (EC) was concerned about the competitive advantages that Universal was seeking. They were worried that Universal was already the biggest force in the industry, and the addition of EMI would make it even bigger. With less competition, digital platforms would feel the financial pinch as Universal-EMI created favorable licensing agreements. The digital platforms would in turn pass on cost increases to European consumers, something that the EC wanted to avoid.

To satisfy the regulators, Universal would divest $680 million in "non-core assets." It had to sell the iconic label Parlophone, EMI France, Chrysalis, Mute, and Coop, a label-licensing business. Universal also committed to avoid Most Favored Nation (MFN) clauses for 10 years in contracts with digital customers. MFN clauses forced customers to extend any favorable term granted to Universal's competitors to Universal, a huge advantage had the EC permitted it.

In the end, Universal's negotiations with the Europeans were enough to allow the acquisition to move forward, and the Commission reported its approval with a brief statement:

> *In light of these commitments, the Commission concluded that competition on the digital music markets in the [European Economic Area] will be adequately*

preserved and that the transaction will have no negative impact on consumers.[10]

Not everyone was happy with the approval. Jeffrey Rabhan, who chaired the Clive Davis Institute of Recorded Music at New York University, said, "From a competitive standpoint, it would have been better for the industry if Warner and E M I had merged. You want to have three strong players, not two and a half."[11] Too bad Warner just didn't have the money or the leadership to pull it off.

Dead Broke: Bankruptcy in Business

I wish I could tell you that every company fights the good fight and that the creditors let them be. I wish I could tell you that, but business is no fairy-tale world.[12] Insufficient funding, bad market conditions, poor leadership, and other factors can gradually creep in or attack suddenly to lay low an organization trying to make a dollar. Hard times can hit wobbly startups in their first years or even take down historic institutions after ages on the scene. Bankruptcy trashes credit, damages professional reputations, and can be personally devastating for the individuals filing.

Fortunately, U S law and financial systems are structured so that when things are bad and there doesn't seem to be any other way out, companies can turn to bankruptcy to stop the pain. It is a legal status that lets an organization sort out its finances and start over. It can hold creditors at bay on some of the most painful actions: repossession, lawsuits, and other types of harassment. Under the protection of bankruptcy, some debts can be discharged or written off. Others may be restructured to get the creditors some or all of the money they are owed over a set period of time. The reprieve that bankruptcy provides allows people and businesses to recover from tough times and fight another day . . . albeit with understandably tarnished credit rating.

It wouldn't be America if we only had one flavor of anything. Businesses have many choices as to how they incorporate, such as sole proprietorships, partnerships, limited liability companies, and corporations, to name a few. With that kind of variety, naturally there would be at least as many categories in the United States Bankruptcy Code, but the most common types of debt relief the law allows are Chapter 7, Chapter 13, and Chapter 11. Each type offers advantages, disadvantages, and restrictions on eligibility. The complexity of the process is such that it is worth an executive's time to get expert advice and legal support weighing the pros and cons of bankruptcy options. Don't make going broke worse than it has to be.

Chapter 7 is a common type of bankruptcy for small businesses. Although the owner may elect Chapter 7, sometimes the court will make that choice for him or her, especially in cases where there is limited asset value in the business and little or no income. It liquidates assets and generally ends the business. The intent is to use the money from the liquidation to pay debts that continue in existence despite the bankruptcy, such as professional bankruptcy processing fees, the tax bill (Uncle Sam is always close to the front of the line), and tax liens.[13]

The structure of the company has a lot to do with what can be saved in bankruptcy. Corporations and limited liability companies treat the owners and the organization as separate entities, and that protects the owner's personal assets from seizure in the event of the corporation's default on most debts. That protection goes right out the window if owners make the mistake of mixing their personal finances with the corporation's finances. If there isn't a strong distinction, the courts may roll personal assets in with the failing business.

Sole proprietorships and partnerships are on the hook for virtually everything they have when finances go south, but those personal guarantees are one of the things that attract creditors to loan them money.[14] People filing for Chapter 7 can exempt some of their assets from liquidation. What will survive the fire sale depends on state laws and the value of the assets. An owner might be able to save a house in one place but not in another. Unless the bling of household goods and clothing are worthy of a celebrity show-off program like *MTV Cribs*, those items are usually exempt.

Sugar Hill Records was the first record label to launch a successful Hip-Hop single with "Rapper's Delight," introducing Rap music to the mass market. Having achieved gold status with half a million records sold, Sugar Hill made history for the new musical genre and made money for the label owners, Joe and Sylvia Robinson. However, things didn't stay rosy for Sugar Hill for very long.

> *. . . Sugar Hill Records' swift decline was largely of their own making . . . Part of it was hubris . . . Part of it was greed . . . Part of it was ignorance . . . Part of it was recklessness.*[15]

The Robinsons refused good potential partners in favor of shady gangster types. They failed to recognize changes in the audience's musical tastes and adapt A&R activities accordingly. They "even rejected a free video for 'White Lines' made by a young student filmmaker at New York University named Spike Lee," who would go on to do great things in film.[16] The Robinsons never saw a personal expense they didn't like, and they never saw an artist's financial claim as a valid obligation for compensation. Sugar Hill did almost nothing for artist development, a fact that allowed Russell Simmons' and Rick Rubin's Def Jam Records to swoop in as Sugar Hill faltered.

> *. . . the hit records covered a multitude of sins—sins revealed when the hits dried up. Sugar Hill spent too*

much and made too little. Now it needed money. Joe and Sylvia Robinson faced financial ruin.[17]

The Robinsons had filed for bankruptcy before. In this particular incident, they did not technically file for Chapter 7 bankruptcy. However, what happened to them and Sugar Hill Records was remarkably similar. CBS Records refused to provide any funding to the Robinsons. Two labels, Capitol Records and CBS, valued the catalog of master tapes, the treasure chest of any record label's assets, at one-tenth of what Sugar Hill had it as on the books—$500,000 rather than $5 million. That left the Robinsons with no meaningful collateral to secure new loans or pay existing debts. Finally, two mob-connected axmen stepped in. Morris Levy and Salvatore Pisello arranged a deal that transferred the masters to MCA Records to cover previous losses and ongoing manufacturing costs. Sugar Hill Records and the Robinsons were finished.

Chapter 13 is the bankruptcy option for individuals and companies with relatively limited debt coupled with sufficient assets, resources, and future potential to stay in business. The law prohibits corporations and partnerships from this type of filing. Additionally, there are modest upper limits to the assets a company or individual can have when considering Chapter 13: below $400,000 in unsecured debts and less than $1.2 million in secured debt. Courts set repayment rates and direct them to parties in accordance with the priority of the type of debt. Unsecured debts have fewer protections for the debt holders, and payment to these creditors is set at least as high as the rate that they would have received if the debtor's assets were liquidated under the rules of Chapter 7 bankruptcy. Still, that provides some savings to the person or organization seeking Chapter 13 protections.

One of the worst parts of life in the lead-up to bankruptcy is the relentless calls from creditors demanding payment. Chapter 13 can halt this painful, anxiety-provoking, and humiliating aspect of financial difficulties. A trustee, the law's representative to facilitate and enforce the conditions of the bankruptcy, acts as the intermediary between the debtor and creditors. The debtor pays the trustee, and the trustee pays the creditors. The harassment generally stops while under Chapter 13 protection.

Chapter 13 sets a three- to five-year repayment schedule that the debtor pays in installments. Individuals and organizations get to keep the property for which they are making the more-manageable payments agreed to as part of the bankruptcy. That framework is critical to organizations that want to get back on their feet. However, like any bankruptcy arrangement, regardless of the chapter, it requires better luck, effort, and discipline of the company and its staff than existed before the filing. Debtors must make all their payments in full and on time, or the protections afforded by the bankruptcy vanish.

Because of its potential to protect personal assets like super mansions, tricked-out supercars, and gold-plated firearms from the humiliation of repossession, Chapter 13 has been a favorite avenue for rappers to get out from underneath crushing debts. California rapper Micheal Ray "Tyga" Stevenson is best known for hits like "Hookah" and "Switch Lane." However, before he managed to draw millions of fans, releasing albums through a high-profile Hip-Hop label like Young Money, Tyga put out a lukewarm studio album called *No Introduction* through Decaydance Records. Although the recording got Tyga's music out into the world, it didn't make him terribly rich.

In fact, Tyga had difficulties meeting the expenses of even a lower-tier rapper. Despite his limited income at the time, he managed to rack up the significant debts of a big baller. When the bills for his posh Tarzana home in L.A. became too much for him in late 2010, Tyga filed for Chapter 13 bankruptcy, claiming that he only had $50,000, a figure far short of the $500,000 he owed. That wasn't a bad move.

However, one of his primary creditors, HSBC Bank USA, claimed that a $700,000 debt on a home in Whittier, California, was transferred between parties in violation of the terms of the bankruptcy. HSBC argued that house should have been included in the repayment plan or allowed to proceed into foreclosure.

> *The bankruptcy filing was dismissed in February, and no debt was wiped clean because of the Young Money rapper's failure to provide the required documents.*[18]

Money troubles suck. Bankruptcy is hard. Nevertheless, screwing around with shady asset transfers during a financial crisis is a terrible idea. Tyga was ultimately able to pay off his debts with the revenue from the hits he created after 2010, but more controlled spending and disciplined administrative work during the bankruptcy process would have saved Tyga a lot of trouble. He might have come up with a better title for the sophomore album he released around the time of his bankruptcy. *Careless World* sounded a bit too autobiographical . . .

Chapter 11 is the legal filing people think of when they hear the word "bankruptcy." It is the common refuge of corporations and partnerships, and like Chapter 13, it is intended to reorganize a business and pay creditors over time. However, it is costly, complicated, and time consuming, which is why larger organizations have an easier time pulling it off compared to smaller operations. General Motors, Marvel Entertainment, and United Airlines all had their turn under its protective umbrella. The organization filing Chapter 11 creates a strategy that trims costs, finds new revenue sources, and plans a return to profitability, all while keeping debt holders at bay. The debtor is required to make monthly operating reports to the court as proof that the payments are on time and that the reorganization is on the path to commercial success and financial solvency.

Reorganization sets new liability payments based on reduced values to creditors. It allows companies to renegotiate contracts with suppliers and even labor unions. The unions and suppliers frequently go along with the negotiations, based on the belief that it is better for the company to remain in business and get something rather than insist on the previous terms and see the company go out of business altogether. The devil that you know is better than the devil that you don't.

Robert F.X. Sillerman was a media and entertainment entrepreneur who enjoyed his fair share of success in business. In 1993, he created SFX Entertainment, a concert and stage performance promoter, and he did well enough with that venture that he was able to sell the operation to Clear Channel Communication in 2000 for $4.4 billion. Pretty respectable. Clear Channel would spin off the business as the world's premier event coordinating company, Live Nation. Sillerman liked what he did, so he created a new version of SFX Entertainment that would also do event promotion like the 2015 Summer Set Music Festival that featured Hip-Hop acts Ghostface Killah, Action Bronson, Earl Sweatshirt, G-Eazy, Bone Thugs-N-Harmony, F. Stokes, Keys N Krates, Lil Dicky, Mike Floss, WebsterX, ishDARR, and Saba.[19]

Even though SFX Entertainment could attract good, if not great, Hip-Hop talent to its events, it was no Live Nation. The company's focus on electronic music events denied it the wider audience that the original SFX Entertainment and its later incarnations enjoyed. Furthermore, Sillerman's leadership as CEO wasn't what it used to be 20 years earlier. Although he and SFX staff tried to generate value and grow the business, the cost of operations outstripped the revenues from events. Sillerman made two unusual and unsuccessful attempts to buy out stockholders, which only generated greater frustration in light of sagging profitability. Without many other good options, Sillerman took SFX Entertainment into Chapter 11.

As is often the case, a company's debt holders and investors do not quietly acquiesce to the bath they have to take in bankruptcy proceedings. SFX's case required amendments to address the concerns of unsecured creditors to whom the company owed $367 million. The original filing attempted to waive the stakeholders' rights to sue Sillerman, board members, and other officers involved in SFX's decline and shady dealings. SFX's reorganization plan intended to provide creditors stock or equity stakes in the new company, but their minority position in a privately held company was of little actual market value. Creditors could reasonably ask who would want to buy a few shares of an unprofitable event-promotion company, and why would they expect a fair price for that stock if they tried to sell it? Creditors pushed back against the SFX plan, and the courts agreed to changes. As a final blow to Sillerman for his failures as CEO, investors and creditors insisted he step down as CEO following reorganization.[20] When SFX Entertainment emerged from Chapter 11 having freed itself of $400 million dollars in debt, the new CEO, Randy Phillips, renamed the company LiveStyle, viewing the old name as too tarnished and too closely associated with its disgraced former CEO, Robert F.X. Sillerman. Bankruptcy, and the drama that goes with it, is a tough way to end your professional existence.

Mic Drop: Exit Strategies

Business is like a train ride. Whether someone steps down at the first stop just a little while after starting or they ride until the end of the line, at some point, everyone has got to get off. Owners and executives need to plan the end game for their businesses. Winding down operations, transferring ownership or control, and moving on to greener pastures is a natural part of the business life cycle. The better planned that process is, the smoother things go for the stakeholders, the people who provided value to and derived value from the company, and the higher the chances are for a good final payday. There are plenty of ways to play out the endgame and get money back out of the business. Business author and venture coach, Stever Robbins, grouped exit strategies into five classes: extracting income, liquidation, the friendly sale, third-party acquisition, and the IPO.[21]

Extracting cash from the business is popular with Ballers-in-Chief interested in maintaining a lifestyle rather than growing the company. Owners can treat the organization like a personal piggy bank by drawing ginormous salaries, giving themselves huge bonuses, and creating special stock classification with sick dividend payouts. Yes, it's all candy-colored supercars, jet-set world travel, and gold-lined designer track suits for the titleholders looking to enjoy the finer things in life while the business is in operation. The gravy train can keep on rolling just as long as the business stays in operation. However, as hard as it is to believe, there are downsides to raping and pillaging a business like a Roman legionnaire besides the pulmonary edema associated with snorting too much coke off of strippers' chests.

Cash extraction can limit or halt a company's ability to grow, since all the operating profits are going into the owner's wallet. Things like capital expenditure, research and development, and salaries for high-quality talent needed to compete and expand in the market are off the table when the money goes out the door. That can frustrate employees, anger investors, leave the business vulnerable to decline, and prevent the possibility of passing it on in the family without careful management. It is probably not an option for publicly traded companies subject to the rules and regulations of the SEC and FTC, but owners of private companies can consider extraction as one type of exit strategy.

Bryan "Birdman" Williams and family haven't been shy about extracting dough from Cash Money Records and its related touring and apparel operations. In a *Forbes* interview with Zack O'Malley Greenburg, Birdman estimated that he and his family took out about $100 million from the company.[22] With full and complete ownership of the companies, the Williams family was in the enviable position to extract wealth at their discretion. Birdman's collection of toys is featured in shows, magazines, and social media video streams featuring his Miami Beach mansion, Bugatti Veyron, Lamborghini Veneno 5, Lamborghini Adventador, Maybach Exelero, Maybach Ladaulet, and Mercedes-Benz S65 AMG, just to name a few.

To their credit, the Williams family have managed the business well even as they enjoy the economic fruits of the business. However, none of it would have been possible without Birdman's shrewd leadership and wise decision to leave enough operating income in the business to grow it from a small Louisiana storefront into a $300 million operation and one of Hip-Hop's most important music institutions. If he hadn't, he and the Williamses might not have quite so much bling, and the world might never have heard the music of Cash Money's artists like Lil Wayne, Drake, Nicki Minaj, Tyga, and DJ Khaled.

Another option for owners looking to end it all is an old-fashioned fire sale. Closing up shop and liquidating assets is a quintessential mic-dropping moment in business. It is definitive and unambiguous. Uncle Sam gets paid taxes and fees. Agreements are cancelled. Creditors and suppliers get their final payments. Final customer collections come in. Client lists are either sold off or cast aside. Inventory, supplies, plant, and equipment all go to the highest bidder. Employees collect their belongings, vacation, sick pay, and benefits payouts, and head out the door. Whatever is left after all of that is divided among the stockholders. All the things that used to make up the business evaporate.

This endgame strategy is unpopular, since it rarely generates the largest return. It would seem to be a shame to see resources, processes, and personnel organized to do business cashed in for the market value of residual assets.

> *Things like client lists, your reputation, and your business relationships may be very valuable, and liquidation just destroys them without an opportunity to recover their value.*[23]

Executives doing their jobs well can usually get more for the sum of the whole rather than for the auction value of components sold separately. However, sometimes an industry can go sour, reducing or eliminating better alternatives like selling out. For owners committed to the liquidation route, there are businesses like *Liquidation.com* dedicated to getting the most value for the owners in the sale process . . . for a cut of the proceeds.

If you grew up in the Rocky Mountains, Great Plains, or Midwestern states, you might remember Hastings Entertainment, a consumer electronics company specializing in music, video, and gaming retail establishments. The record store was founded in 1972, before the birth of Hip-Hop, growing to 123 stores around the US at the time that it was sold off in pieces in mid-2016. Hastings was there selling Hip-Hop music in vinyl, cassette tapes, and CDs as the genre picked up speed and changed media over the 1980s, '90s, and early 2000s. But business changed with the arrival of the Internet. The stores saw their business shrink as digital media, online sales, and streaming services came at the expense of bricks-and-mortar retailers.

With no meaningful way to turn the business around and no good competitors willing to buy them out, Hastings decided to sell everything and shut down. Hilco Merchant Recourses and Gordon Brothers Retail Partners were on the scene to sell off the company's assets.

. . . the Hastings chain has about $140 million in inventory; about $70 million is owed to secured creditors . . . Another $50 million is owed to unsecured creditors . . .[24]

Despite the inventory's purported value of $140 million, the best bid the liquidators received was for about $95 million, and that left only "about $25 million to be split among the other unsecured creditors,"[25] since the $70 million in secured credit was paid first in the event of default.

Hastings' end was sad, and it teaches a few lessons: Business must adapt to changing industry trends. The liquidation process doesn't get every dime a business thinks it's worth. Never carry too much Chief Keef, JR Smith, or Young Thug music in your inventory, because that crap will never sell.

Owners who value continuity for the business after their departure can look for a friendly buyer. Like-minded buyers are likely to maintain a company's culture, key personnel, market strategy, operational locations, or other sacred cows that an owner would want to know go on with the new administration. The best candidates for a friendly buyout could be family members or company employees who are familiar with how things have gone at the business and theoretically would like to see them continue. Other possible options are suppliers or customers whose relationships were important to the company's success.[26] The process allows the owner to remain in control of succession and some conditions of the sale.

This exit strategy is more lucrative than a liquidation, but the short list of possible friendly buyers almost guarantees that the payout will be smaller or take longer than if the entire market, loaded with fat investment banks, high-rolling private equity firms, and stanky-rich venture capitalists bid to purchase the company. It's just simple supply and demand. Even friendly buyers will have ideas and opinions of their own about the business. Squabbling executives and managers enfranchised through an employee stock ownership plan (ESOP) or dysfunctional sibling rivalries in a family business can derail the idyllic vision a departing owner may have had for the corporation after selling out. Sometimes familiarity with an organization and even skin in the game isn't enough for successful power transitions.

Most Hip-Hop fans love listening to deejays create sick beats and layer killer electronic sounds on their gear. The infinite variability of synthesizers and support equipment adds life and character to the music even before emcees and rappers add their artistic contributions. Moog Music was the Asheville, North Carolina-based electronic-instrument manufacturer who helped Dr. Dre and the Beastie Boys with some of Hip-Hop's hottest jams. Although the equipment isn't the most visible part of Hip-Hop, plenty of Hip-Hop would have sounded lifeless without the help of high-quality sound equipment like the Moog Voyager, Moog Model 15 Limited-edition Reissue Modular Synthesizer, Polymoog, Minimoog, Moog Sub Phatty 25-Key Analog Monophonic Synthesizer, Memorymoog, and Moog Little Phatty.

Mike Adams, Moog Music's CEO, loved his job. Who wouldn't love being a foundational part of music creation? Still, despite his role and Moog's iconic status in electronic music, in 2015 Adams decided it was time to plan out his endgame. Gathering his 60-odd full-time employees together, he announced that he was selling half the company to people he believed would do right by Moog Music: the company's workers. Employee Stock Ownership Plans (ESOP) gave 49 percent of the company stock directly to eligible employees. Adams created a trust, loaning the workers money to pay Adams for his last 51 percent over a six-year period. Adams would continue as CEO until the end of the buyout period.[27]

In order to get in on the deal (or "vest," as it's called), an employee would need to work at Moog for six years. In theory, as the company grows and increases in value, so does the stock that the workers would own.

> *If the company continues to grow—[Year to Date] revenue is up nearly 50 percent over 2014 and they've gone from 27 to 62 full-time employees in the past five years—then a production worker with a decade of experience stands to receive an estimated $100,000 payout at retirement age, the company said.*[28]

The ESOP was a good deal for the employees, since their stock ownership gave them equity in their work. Mike Adams got a nice payday when he cashed out half his stock, and if Moog expands with additional sales to Hip-Hop and electronic artists, the payout for his second 51 percent should be even bigger.

The third-party acquisition opens up the competition to sell the company to the whole wide world. The main objective is to negotiate the highest sale price possible, frequently based on a multiplication factor or multiple of the company's Earnings Before Interest, Taxes, Depreciation and Amortization (EBITDA). Owners should work to make their company as attractive as possible for sale by affecting EBITDA. They can make changes to show higher revenues through increased sales, and lower costs through operational efficiencies or deferring expenses. These factors can be used to increase the multiples at the time of sale. There are non-EBITDA factors that can make the business more valuable in a sale, such as stable customer accounts with long-term contracts, acquiring strategic technologies, and developing valuable intellectual property such as patents or trade secrets.

Finding a good buyer isn't impossible. Sometimes it's not hard at all. Competitors might love to sweep up the customer list, product lines, and workforce, or just take a rival business off the street. Other buyers from outside the industry may view the business as a strategic acquisition that fits into a larger business plan. Just as with real estate sales, there are professional brokers who can help connect buyers with sellers for a fee. They can use their networks to drum up activity and potentially spark a bidding war between buyers to jack up the sale price even higher.[29]

Def Jam Records was in an interesting position. Russell Simmons and Lyor Cohen were running the label, which had produced the Beastie Boys, Run-DMC, Public Enemy, and EPMD. PolyGram Records, a Dutch entertainment company with acts like Barry White and Def Leopard, bought 50 percent of Def Jam for $33 million. The move was something that provided PolyGram with access to increasingly popular groups in the American market. Getting control of the rest of Def Jam's stock was a strategic acquisition for the label, and they were willing to negotiate to make that happen.

As part of the arrangement, Def Jam's founders had a buy-sell agreement built in as a way to cash out of the business they built. PolyGram believed that the deal would encourage Simmons and Cohen to hustle hard, managing artists, producing records, and generally growing sales since they would collect a larger payout when the final calculations were complete a few years later.

As acquisitions went, Def Jam's sale was not a typical open-market purchase, where any company could offer to buy the label. The buy-sell agreement with PolyGram created a formula of multiples based on Def Jam album sales.

> *The higher the multiple was, the higher the sale price would be . . . PolyGram might have missed the significance of one crucial deal point: The multiple was based not on profits, but on revenue. In other words, Def Jam's sale price was tied to how many units they sold, not how much they spent to get there.*[30]

PolyGram's mistake would be Simmons' and Cohen's gain. The music entrepreneurs cranked out albums for Def Jam at breakneck speeds. Where other labels were a little more choosy about what projects to do or when to release music, Cohen pushed the artists to work overtime to produce new albums, even schlocky movie soundtracks of dubious quality. Cohen even demanded that DMX, no model of professional discipline, produce a new album with two months' notice.

"As 1998 ended, Lyor Cohen and his team looked back. Def Jam, in one year, had done an unprecedented $175 million in billing for its corporate parent."[31] Those sales, as unprofitable or marginally profitable as they had been, were still counted toward the $100 million payday that Cohen and Simmons enjoyed when they sold their remaining stake in Def Jam to PolyGram. If you're going to sell out, it's nice to have incentives to make it well worth your while.

Why sell a company to another company when you can sell to everyone in the free world? The Initial Public Offering, or IPO, turns privately held shares of an organization's stock and makes them publicly available for sale through stock exchanges like the New York Stock Exchange (NYSE) or the National Association of Securities Dealers Automated Quotations, better known by its acronym, NASDAQ. Only about 7,000 companies are public in the United States.[32] Rather than a single purchasing institution setting a price for the company and buying it, the IPO allows the wisdom of the market to establish and change the price of a company's shares in real time as if it were an auction. Usually, when a company's organization, product offerings, and financial results are attractive, share prices will rise, allowing stockholders to sell their interests for higher returns or collect larger dividends if the new public company offers them.

Although they are sexy, IPOs are no guarantee of a successful and profitable endgame for owners. The effort and expense involved in filing the appropriate paperwork with the Financial Industry Regulatory Authority, Securities and Exchange

Commission, or Federal Trade Commission is daunting. Even once complete, the regulatory requirements to remain compliant with laws like Sarbanes-Oxley, which requires significant and frequent reporting, are intensive and time consuming for the organization.

Before the shares are ever offered, company leaders will need to create a sales pitch and make it to institutional investors just to set the highly changeable opening price. Even all-encompassing and inescapable Facebook had a rough start with its IPO when share prices dropped by more than half from the original price offered for them for a meaningful stretch of time. CEO Mark Zuckerberg couldn't have been too happy with the highly critical market analysts who waffled on their hot-or-not determinations of his company's value . . . and share price. Robbins reminds us of one more kick in the junk about this exit strategy:

> *We won't even talk about the need to conform to Sarbanes-Oxley, or the 6 percent underwriting fees you'll pay to investment bankers, or lockout periods, or how down markets can tank your wealth despite having a healthy business, or how IPO-raised funds distort your income statement, or . . .*[33]

There is no question that the barriers to successful IPOs are significant, but they are not insurmountable. Brave owners can still consider it one of their endgame options.

Although business is part of Hip-Hop culture, IPOs were practically unheard of in the Hip-Hop community. The Real Hip-Hop Network, Inc. hoped to be an exception to that rule. RHN considered itself to be the first 24-hour cable channel and digital media company that focused exclusively on Hip-Hop lifestyle and culture. It produced artist interviews, news, and documentaries that targeted the sweet spot of Hip-Hop's spending demographic, 18- to 34-year-olds. In late 2013, the company's

CEO, Atonn Muhammad, hoped to use an IPO as a method to raise $25 million to grow the business . . . and make a nice piece of change on the side for the sale of some of his shares.

There was reason for hope. The multi-billion dollar Hip-Hop industry circled the globe, and RHN estimated that, in addition to the genre's cradle in the United States, there were an additional 164,000,000 households in Africa, Europe, and the Middle East hungry for Hip-Hop programming. The company had exclusive rights to 30,000 hours of video content. If it worked out, affiliate fees and advertising revenue could slosh around RHN investors like water in an overfilled bathtub.

Unfortunately for RHN, the IPO never seemed to get off the ground. The reasons for the difficulties come into clear focus when reading the reports available on the NASDAQ website. Investors didn't see a bright future for RHN, and the company's prospectus didn't sugarcoat the situation: "Investing in our common stock involves a high degree of risk."[34] There were long-established, well-financed, formidable competitors like MTV, BET, TV One, VH1, and FUSE already successfully competing for the same audiences. RHN was uncertain of its ability to attract and retain consumers. There were questions about the quality and breadth of the content library, especially for Hip-Hop fans, who demand fresh, new content constantly. Finally, even in its short time in business, RHN had a history of financial losses, and it could not guarantee that it would be profitable in the future.

RHN's IPO didn't go anywhere, but clearly Muhammad and his team worked hard to make a case for the company to go public. Fortunately, at $16,889 in offering expenses, they didn't break the bank with costs relating to the IPO.

CHECK-OUT TIME: CONCLUSION

HIP-HOP DESERVES GREATER appreciation for the business lessons it has to offer. Artists, entrepreneurs, enthusiasts, and others created a vibrant culture that opened up new forms of expression, made the world more interesting, and made a bunch of people very rich since its birth. How it went so long without more recognition is stunning.

The origin stories for some of the biggest Hip-Hop stars show ample similarities between their rise and the keys to success that launched economic giants like Google or Amazon. Drake's meteoric rise to the top of the charts showed the same passion to succeed in a creative enterprise as the empire building of Steve Jobs, founder of Apple. Eminem's goal to get out of Detroit on a tide of Hip-Hop success was no less ambitious than Facebook CEO Mark Zuckerberg's mission "to give people the power to share and make the world more open and connected." Hip-Hop entrepreneurs like David Mays and Jonathan Shecter proved that they could plan and operate a media business every bit as well as and frequently better than their mainstream competition at Time Inc.

The salesmanship, marketing prowess, and nose for profit of Snoop Dogg and 50 Cent as drug dealers compare favorably against their larger pharmaceutical competitors like Pfizer and Merck. P Diddy could have taught networking superstar Dale Carnegie a thing or two had the author of the best seller *How to Win Friends and Influence People* not chickened out and died in 1955. The Wu-Tang Clan could have schooled Microsoft on complementary products and blanketing a market with their strategy to distribute diverse, affiliated bands to cover the entire Hip-Hop spectrum. Even Donald Trump's real estate enterprises might not have filed bankruptcy six times if he'd had the property savvy of Biggie Smalls when it came to locating and running businesses.

Communicating like a boss, Akon delivered bad news about missing one of Hip-Hop's biggest acts, and even Ice Cube valued engagement enough to connect with his fans over *Wired*'s cheesy online interviews. Lil Wayne and T.I. could instruct the Society for Human Resource Management on how to run bonus programs from their experience at Cash Money and Arista Records. Hip-Hop management lessons are there for all to see, even when good businesspeople should have chosen a different path. Suge Knight's warped ethics, creative accounting, and gross mismanagement cratered Death Row Records in a similar way and around the same time as Kenneth Lay brought energy giant Enron down in flames in 2001.

Eazy-E and Prodigy learned hard lessons from their poor hiring decisions of band managers, which cost them millions in bad contracts and lost revenue. However, they didn't do any worse than Kmart hiring the do-nothing Chuck Conway, who took the ailing retailer straight down the smokestack. L.A.'s Power 106 station's staff set the standard for cultural training just prior to the 1992 riots. Both major American political parties could stand to replicate Power's outreach, given their inability to reach beyond the walls of their ideological fortresses to people outside their parochial cliques. Eminem showed that adding diversity to a team could have huge benefits for an organization willing to deal with its challenges.

If project management is how to get a job done, Hip-Hop greats have it down cold. Well, not all of them . . . DMX serves as a walking cautionary tale with his nonexistent planning and sloppy contracting. Ice-T, on the other hand, dominated the robbery game with thorough planning and careful risk management. RZA knew how to budget to make Wu-Wear one of the most successful merchandising programs in music . . . at least more profitable than the KISS Kasket, the heavy-metal-themed repository for deceased rockers. KISS apparently didn't do project management.

When it comes to finance, Hip-Hop could easily battle against Adam Smith and his *Wealth of Nations*. Dee-1 proved rules on credit allocation and debt service with his student loans, rules that Tyco International and WorldCom could have learned from to avoid the dumpster fires they became. Priority Records founders Cory Robbins and Steve Plotnicki did a better job with startup financing with their $34,000 launching some the biggest names in early Hip-Hop than Digital Convergence with its useless barcode scanner, CueCat, which still tanked after $185 million in capital. Queen Latifah might have learned about tax payments the hard way, but unlike Starbucks, Apple, Ikea, and Google, her deferral plan arranged with the IRS didn't bring thousands of protesters into the street for dubious revenue maneuvers.

Maybe because of their hustler worldview, the Hip-Hop set are well suited to weather major change in business. Russell Simmons gambled and won with his risks at Def Jam Recordings, Phat Farm, and Baby Phat to build a $340 million empire. Tyga, like 66 percent of those filing Chapter 13 bankruptcy, didn't do too well with it, but he was able to bounce back with the revenue from later commercial successes. Jay-Z's sale of Roc-A-Fella Records to Universal Music Group was just one way to cash out of a business position. Birdman found a happy medium when it came to extracting cash from Cash Money for his exit strategy.

I don't know about you, but everything I need to know about business I learned from Hip-Hop.

SHOUT-OUTS: ACKNOWLEDGEMENTS

I WOULD LIKE TO ACKNOWLEDGE and thank the rappers, DJs, emcees, producers, A&R professionals, writers, engineers, artists, technicians, managers, and executives whose contributions make Hip-Hop music possible. While the big ballers have their piles of cash to keep them warm, many do not get the appreciation and thanks that they deserve for their work. If there is one thing that I've learned over my career, it is that it takes the whole team to get a job done right.

I could not have written this book without the excellent work of other authors, journalists, bloggers, and Hip-Hop enthusiasts. They added tremendously to my understanding of the music, culture, and characters of the genre and brought Hip-Hop to life for me. Their writing made my research much more interesting, and they helped me tell stories and illustrate business concepts that I hope you've enjoyed.

I've been lucky to have excellent support from friends, coworkers, and fans of the genre. Shout-out to Ben Davis, Jacob Todd, Sean Kenzel, Brandon Vice, and Barry Edwards in the Joint Interface Control Cell. Their energy and attitude kept me going. Mark Mathis deserves credit for laughing with me on different

Hip-Hop/business concepts mash-ups. There is a special thank you to Dan Landis, Ken Bauer, and Bill Herdrich for their insight on finance, management, and support for the project. I owe Dr. Marwa El Mourabet for some of the best humor in the text.

I was lucky to have an excellent writing coach, Derek Lewis, whose professional advice helped me move this book from a hazy patchwork of ideas into the completed work you are reading. Any writer would be fortunate to have his tremendous experience and guidance.

I would also like to thank my family for their support throughout the process. I'd like to call out for special thanks my father, Bert Miller, whose leadership carried our company through tough times to growth and prosperity. The best lessons here I learned from him. Finally, there is my brother, Alby Miller, who helped create the idea for the book.

ENDNOTES

Chapter 1

[1]   Dan Charnas, *The Big Payback: The History of the Business of Hip-Hop.* (New York: New American Library/Penguin Group, 2010), 445

[2]   Setaro, Shawn. "Baby Money: Inside the Early Years of Birdman's Cash Money Records" *Forbes.* Forbes, Inc. 5 May 2015. Web.11 Apr 2016

[3]   Forbes. *Ibid.*

[4]   Russell Simmons with Chris Morrow, *Do You! 12 Laws to Access the Power in You to Achieve Happiness and Success.* (New York: Gotham Books 2007), 26–27

[5]   Simmons, *Ibid.* 26–27

[6]   "Hip-Hop Association." *Play.fm.* n.p., n.d. Web. 27 Jan. 2017.

[7]   "Nicki Minaj." *Wikipedia.* Wikimedia Foundation, n.d. Web. 27 Oct. 2016.

[8]   Richmond, Annette. "Stop Dreaming & Start Doing: Smart Goals Are Your Key to Success" *Career-Intelligence.* Career-Intelligence.com LLC. n.d. 1 Nov. 2016.

[9]   Marshall B Mathers III, *Eminem: The Way I Am* (New York, NY: Dutton, 2008), 144–146.

[10]   Mathers, *Ibid.* 110

[11]   James Haskins, *One Nation Under a Groove: Rap Music and Its Roots* (New York, NY: Hyperion Books for Children, 2000), 39–52

[12]   "Recording Industry Association of America" *Wikipedia.* Wikimedia Foundation, n.d. Web. 4 Nov. 2016.

[13] "Rapper's Delight." *Wikipedia.* Wikimedia Foundation, n.d. Web. 27 Oct. 2016.

[14] Marshall B Mathers III, *Eminem: The Way I Am* (New York, NY: Dutton, 2008), 22.

[15] Mathers, *Ibid.* 128

[16] "How Tall Is the Average NBA Player?" *ChaCha.* ChaCha, Inc. n.d. 24 Sep 2015.

[17] Queen Latifah with Samantha Marshall, *Put on Your Crown: Life-Changing Moments on the Path to Queendom* (New York, NY: Grand Central Publishing, 2010), 60

[18] Latifah with Marshall, *Ibid.* 67

[19] Curtis James Jackson, *From Pieces to Weight: Once Upon a Time in Southside Queens* (New York, NY: Pocket Books, 2005), 51

[20] Jackson, *Ibid.* 34

[21] Tayannah Lee McQuillar and Fred L. Johnson III, PhD, *Tupac Shakur: The Life and Times of an American Icon* (Cambridge: Da Capo Press 2010), 189

[22] Dan Charnas, *The Big Payback: The History of the Business of Hip-Hop.* (New York: New American Library/Penguin Group, 2010), 263–264

[23] Charnas, *Ibid.* 264

[24] Selby, Jenn. "Rapper Rick Ross Wins $10 Million Court Battle Against Former Drug Kingpin to Keep His Name." *The Independent.* Independent Digital News and Media, 2 Jan. 2014. Web. 14 Sep. 2016.

[25] *"Teflon Don* (Album)." *Wikipedia.* Wikimedia Foundation, n.d. Web. 18 Oct. 2016.

Chapter 2

[1] Ahmir "Questlove" Thompson and Ben Greenman, *Mo' Meta Blues: The World According to Questlove.* (New York: Grand Central Publishing 2013), 171

[2] "Miami Vice." *Wikipedia.* Wikimedia Foundation, n.d. Web. 18 Oct. 2016.

[3] Ben Westhoff, *Dirty South: Outkast, Lil Wayne, Soulja Boy, and the Southern Rappers Who Reinvented Hip-Hop.* (Chicago: Chicago Review Press 2011), 175

[4] Westhoff, *Ibid.* 174

⁵ Tayannah Lee McQuillar and Fred L. Johnson III, PhD, *Tupac Shakur: The Life and Times of an American Icon* (Cambridge: Da Capo Press 2010), 181–182

⁶ Zack O'Malley Greenburg, *Empire State of Mind: How Jay-Z Went from Street Corner to Corner Office.* (New York: Penguin Group 2011) 193–194

⁷ Jake Brown, *Ready to Die: The Story of Biggie Smalls.* (Phoenix: Colossus Books 2004), 7

⁸ Brown, *Ibid.* 93

⁹ Brown, *Ibid.* 92–93

¹⁰ Dan Charnas, *The Big Payback: The History of the Business of Hip-Hop.* (New York: New American Library/Penguin Group, 2010), 298

¹¹ Charnas, *Ibid.* 295

¹² Jake Brown, *Ready to Die: The Story of Biggie Smalls.* (Phoenix: Colossus Books 2004), 38.

¹³ Snoop Dogg also did an excellent job picking out his drug-dealing location in Long Beach at Sixty-First Street and Atlantic Avenue, a major north-south artery at the north end of town. The site was less than a mile away from exit 12A of CA-91, the closest highway, making it easy for customers driving from other parts of town. It was also just a block south of the three-acre green space at Houghton Park, meaning the location was great for foot traffic, too. It isn't impossible to imagine either Biggie's or Snoop's locations as the sites of Starbucks if the crime rate was lower and the income rates were higher for the corporate coffee giant . . .

¹⁴ Albert "Prodigy" Johnson with Laura Checkoway, *My Infamous Life*: The Autobiography of Mobb Deep's Prodigy. (New York: Touchstone, 2011), 143

¹⁵ Johnson with Checkoway, *Ibid.* 143

¹⁶ Johnson with Checkoway, *Ibid.* 145

¹⁷ Russell Simmons with Chris Morrow, *Do You! 12 Laws to Access the Power in You to Achieve Happiness and Success.* (New York: Gotham Books 2007) 253–254

¹⁸ Dan Charnas, *The Big Payback: The History of the Business of Hip-Hop.* (New York: New American Library/Penguin Group, 2010), 256

Chapter 3

¹ Jake Brown, *Suge Knight: The Rise, Fall and Rise of Death Row Records.* (Phoenix: Colossus Books 2002), 7

[2]   Ben Westhoff, *Dirty South: Outkast, Lil Wayne, Soulja Boy, and the Southern Rappers Who Reinvented Hip-Hop.* (Chicago: Chicago Review Press 2011), 8–9

[3]   Westhoff, *Ibid.* 8

[4]   Afrizap. "Akon Explains Why He Decided Not to Sign Drake on His Label." – *AFRIZAP WORLD.* n.p., 01 Oct. 2015. Web. 2 Nov. 2016.

[5]   Curtis "50 Cent" Jackson and Kris Ex, *50 Cent: From Pieces to Weight.* (New York: Pocket Books 2005), 44

[6]   50 Cent, *Ibid.* 44

[7]   50 Cent, *Ibid.* 44

[8]   Zack O'Malley Greenburg, *Empire State of Mind: How Jay-Z Went from Street Corner to Corner Office.* (New York: Penguin Group 2011), 3

[9]   Gale, Alex. "T.I. Talks '$200 Million' Major Label Deal & 'G.D.O.D.' Mixtape." *Billboard.* Prometheus Global Media, 10 May 2013. Web. 11 Nov. 2016.

[10]   Book, Ryan. "Biggest Contracts in Music History: Jay-Z, Lil Wayne, Michael Jackson and More." *Music Times.* n.p., 05 Aug. 2015. Web. 27 Nov. 2016.

[11]   Dan Charnas, *The Big Payback: The History of the Business of Hip-Hop.* (New York: New American Library/Penguin Group, 2010), 468–469

[12]   Ben Westhoff, *Dirty South: Outkast, Lil Wayne, Soulja Boy, and the Southern Rappers Who Reinvented Hip-Hop.* (Chicago: Chicago Review Press 2011), 130–131

[13]   Jake Brown, *Suge Knight: The Rise, Fall and Rise of Death Row Records.* (Phoenix: Colossus Books 2002), 90

[14]   Boone, Mary E. & Snowden, David J., "A Leader's Framework for Decision-Making" *HRB.* Harvard Business Press, Nov. 2007. 5 Oct 2016.

[15]   Bonacina, Edoardo. "No need to pay? The impact of piracy on the music industry." *Drayton Tribune.* University College London, n.d. Web. 28 Nov. 2016.

[16]   Ice-T and Douglas Century, *Ice: A Memoir of Gangster Life and Redemption—From South Central to Hollywood.* (New York: One World Books/Random House, 2011), 61–63

[17]   Ahmed, Insanul. "The 20 Most Humiliating Hip-Hop Apologies: Jay-Z's Mom Makes Him Apologize For 'Superugly.'" *Complex.* Complex Media, Inc., 9 Sept. 2011. Web. 28 Nov. 2016.

18 Berry, Eric D. "From Drake to 2 Pac to Wale . . . Rap's Most Emotional Rappers." *HipHollywood*. KevinFrazierProductions.com, 10 July 2014. Web. 3 Dec. 2016.

Chapter 4

1 Ice-T and Douglas Century, *Ice: A Memoir of Gangster Life and Redemption-From South Central to Hollywood*. (New York: One World Books/Random House, 2011), 41

2 Albert "Prodigy" Johnson with Laura Checkoway, *My Infamous Life*: The Autobiography of Mobb Deep's Prodigy. (New York: Touchstone, 2011), 64.

3 Snoop Dogg with Davin Seay, *Tha Doggfather: The Times, Trials, and Hardcore Truths of Snoop Dogg*. (New York: William Morrow and Co. 1999), 50–51

4 Snoop, *Ibid*. 50–51

5 Snoop, *Ibid*. 50–51

6 Dan Charnas, *The Big Payback: The History of the Business of Hip-Hop*. (New York: New American Library/Penguin Group, 2010), 332

7 Charnas, *Ibid*. 333

8 Jake Brown, *Ready to Die: The Story of Biggie Smalls Notorious B.I.G. King of the World & New York City Fast Money, Puff Daddy, Faith and Life After Death: The Unauthorized Biography* (Phoenix: Colossus Books, 2004), 6

9 Brown, *Ibid*. 7

10 Zack O'Malley Greenburg, *Empire State of Mind: How Jay-Z Went from Street Corner to Corner Office*. (New York: Penguin Group 2011), 192

11 The RZA, *The Wu-Tang Manual*. (New York: Berkley Publishing Group 2005), 78

12 Ronin Ro, *Dr. Dre: The Biography* (New York: Thunder's Mouth Press, 2007), 159–160

13 Ro, *Ibid*. 159–160

14 Earl Simmons with Smokey D. Fontaine, E.A.R.L (Ever Always Real Life): *The Autobiography of DMX* (New York: Harper Entertainment 2002), 220

15 DMX, *Ibid*. 214

16 DMX, *Ibid*. 233

17 DMX, *Ibid*. 248–249

[18] Ronin Ro, *Dr. Dre: The Biography* (New York: Thunder's Mouth Press, 2007), 169

[19] Snoop Dogg with Davin Seay, *Tha Doggfather: The Times, Trials, and Hardcore Truths of Snoop Dogg.* (New York: William Morrow and Co. 1999), 74

[20] Albert "Prodigy" Johnson with Laura Checkoway, *My Infamous Life*: The Autobiography of Mobb Deep's Prodigy. (New York: Touchstone, 2011), 184.

[21] Philips, Chuck. "The $50-Million Rap Master: MCA, Andre Harrell Forge Long-Term Multimedia Deal." *Los Angeles Times.* Los Angeles Times, 11 June 1992. Web. 19 Nov. 2016.

Chapter 5

[1] Chase, Zoe "How Much Does It Cost to Make a Hit Song?" *Planet Money.* NPR, 30 Jun 2011. Web. 27 Jan 2017

[2] Ronin Ro, *Dr. Dre: The Biography* (New York: Thunder's Mouth Press, 2007), 4

[3] Ro, *Ibid.* 26

[4] Dan Charnas, *The Big Payback: The History of the Business of Hip-Hop.* (New York: New American Library/Penguin Group, 2010), 484–485

[5] Charnas, *Ibid.* 486

[6] Life, Intelligent. "Bubbles and Bling." *The Economist.* The Economist Group, 08 May 2006. Web. 27 Jan. 2017.

[7] Zack O'Malley Greenburg, *Empire State of Mind: How Jay-Z Went from Street Corner to Corner Office.* (New York: Penguin Group 2011), 122

[8] Earl Simmons with Smokey D. Fontaine, E.A.R.L (Ever Always Real Life): The Autobiography of DMX (New York: Harper Entertainment 2002), 172–173

[9] Curtis "50 Cent" Jackson and Kris Ex, *50 Cent: From Pieces to Weight.* (New York: Pocket Books 2005), 33

[10] Ahmir "Questlove" Thompson and Ben Greenman, *Mo' Meta Blues: The World According to Questlove.* (New York: Grand Central Publishing 2013), 164

[11] Thompson and Greenman, *Ibid.* 167

[12] Queen Latifah with Karen Hunter, *Ladies First: Revelations of a Strong Woman.* (New York: William Morrow and Co, 1999), 54–55

[13] Tayannah Lee McQuillar and Fred L. Johnson III, PhD, *Tupac Shakur: The Life and Times of an American Icon* (Cambridge: Da Capo Press 2010), 77

[14] McQuillar and Johnson, *Ibid.* 78

[15] Dan Charnas, *The Big Payback: The History of the Business of Hip-Hop.* (New York: New American Library/Penguin Group, 2010), 257–258

[16] Ice-T and Douglas Century, *Ice: A Memoir of Gangster Life and Redemption-From South Central to Hollywood.* (New York: One World Books/Random House, 2011), 57

[17] Ice-T and Century, *Ibid.* 58

[18] Zack O'Malley Greenburg, *Empire State of Mind: How Jay-Z Went from Street Corner to Corner Office.* (New York: Penguin Group 2011), 44

Chapter 6

[1] Snoop Dogg with Davin Seay, *Tha Doggfather: The Times, Trials, and Hardcore Truths of Snoop Dogg.* (New York: William Morrow and Co. 1999), 59

[2] Snoop, *Ibid.* 59

[3] Dan Charnas, *The Big Payback: The History of the Business of Hip-Hop.* (New York: New American Library/Penguin Group, 2010), 71

[4] Curtis James Jackson, *From Pieces to Weight: Once Upon a Time in Southside Queens* (New York, NY: Pocket Books, 2005), 34

[5] Snoop Dogg with Davin Seay, *Tha Doggfather: The Times, Trials, and Hardcore Truths of Snoop Dogg.* (New York: William Morrow and Co. 1999), 92–93

[6] Dan Charnas, *The Big Payback: The History of the Business of Hip-Hop.* (New York: New American Library/Penguin Group, 2010), 76

[7] Charnas, *Ibid.* 114–115

[8] Jake Brown, *Suge Knight: The Rise, Fall and Rise of Death Row Records.* (Phoenix: Colossus Books 2002), 53

[9] Brown, *Suge Knight, Ibid.* 22

[10] Brown, *Suge Knight, Ibid.* 54

[11] Sponaugle, Brittani. "Importance of Accounting: Basic Financial Concepts to Know." Udemy Blog. Udemy, Inc., 2 Jan. 2014. Web. 27 Dec. 2016.

[12] Dan Charnas, *The Big Payback: The History of the Business of Hip-Hop.* (New York: New American Library/Penguin Group, 2010), 445

[13] Charnas, *Ibid.* 446–447

[14] "Cash Flow" *BusinessDictionary.com.* WebFinance, Inc., n.d. Web. 17 Dec. 2016.

[15] Queen Latifah and Samantha Marshall, *Put on Your Crown: Life-Changing Moments on the Path to Queendom.* (New York: Grand Central Publishing, 2010), 59–60

[16] "Estimated Taxes." *IRS.GOV.* US Government, 12 Sept. 2016. Web. 28 Dec. 2016.

Chapter 7

[1] Dan Charnas, *The Big Payback: The History of the Business of Hip-Hop.* (New York: New American Library/Penguin Group, 2010), 552

[2] Russell Simmons with Chris Morrow, *Do You! 12 Laws to Access the Power in You to Achieve Happiness and Success.* (New York: Gotham Books 2007) 21–22

[3] Greenburg, Zach O'Malley "Who Killed the Jay-Z Jeep?" *Genius.com,* Genius Media Group, 2012 Web. 9 Jan. 2017.

[4] Queen Latifah with Karen Hunter, *Ladies First: Revelations of a Strong Woman.* (New York: William Morrow and Co, 1999), 4

[5] Weiss, Jeff. "Hip-Hop Lawyer Julian Petty Keeps LA's Top Rappers From Signing Shady Deals" *LA Weekly.* Voice Media Group, 8 Jul 2015. Web. 26 Jan 2017.

[6] Nelson, Chris. "Dr. Dre Warns Napster in Wake of Metallica Lawsuit." *MTV News.* Viacom Media Networks, 18 Apr. 2000. Web. 30 Jan. 2017.

[7] "Tidal (service)." *Wikipedia.* Wikimedia Foundation, n.d. Web. 30 Jan. 2017.

[8] Rys, Dan. "Tidal Sued Again, This Time for Pregnancy Discrimination and Labor Law Violations." *Billboard.* n.p., 23 Nov. 2016. Web. 30 Jan. 2017.

[9] Nicolaou, Anna. "Jay-Z's Tidal sells one-third stake to Sprint for about $200m." *Financial Times.* Financial Times Ltd., 23 Jan. 2017. Web. 21 Mar. 2017.

[10] N.a. "Mergers: Commission Clears Universal's Acquisition of EMI's Recorded Music Business, Subject to Conditions." *European Commission.* European Commission, 21 Sept. 2012. Web. 3 Mar. 2017.

[11] Sisario, Ben. "EMI Is Sold for $4.1 Billion in Combined Deals, Consolidating the Music Industry." *The New York Times*. The New York Times Company, 11 Nov. 2011. Web. 23 Mar. 2017.

[12] *The Shawshank Redemption*, directed by Frank Darabont (1994; Hollywood, CA: Columbia Pictures, 1995), DVD.

[13] QuickBooks. "When Is Bankruptcy the Right Choice?" *QuickBooks*. Intuit Inc., 03 Nov. 2016. Web. 23 Feb. 2017.

[14] QuickBooks, *Ibid*.

[15] Dan Charnas, *The Big Payback: The History of the Business of Hip-Hop*. (New York: New American Library/Penguin Group, 2010), 118

[16] Charnas, *Ibid*. 118

[17] Charnas, *Ibid*. 118

[18] Johnson, Cherise. "Tyga reportedly filed for chapter 13 bankruptcy 5 years ago." *HipHopDX*. Complex Media Inc., 7 Feb. 2016. Web. 23 Feb. 2017.

[19] Shabazz, Sherron. "Win tickets to the 2015 Summer Set Music & Camping Festival." *The Real Hip-Hop*. Real Hip-Hop, LLC, 27 July 2015. Web. 23 Feb. 2017.

[20] Godoy, Jody. "SFX Entertainment Appeases Creditors With New Ch. 11 Plan" *Law360*. Portfolio Media Inc., 14 Sept. 2016. Web. 23 Feb. 2017.

[21] Robbins, Stever. "Exit Strategies for Your Business." *Entrepreneur*. Entrepreneur Media, Inc., 26 June 2005. Web. 25 Feb. 2017.

[22] "Birdman Net Worth: $110 Million In 2016." Interview by Zack O'Malley Greenburg. *Forbes*. Forbes Media LLC, 6 May 2016. Web. 25 Feb. 2017.

[23] Robbins, Stever. "Exit Strategies for Your Business." *Entrepreneur*. Entrepreneur Media, Inc., 26 June 2005. Web. 25 Feb. 2017.

[24] Christman, Ed. "Hastings Entertainment Shutting Down All Stores for Liquidation." *Billboard*. Billboard-Hollywood Reporter Media Group, 21 July 2016. Web. 25 Feb. 2017.

[25] Christman, *Ibid*. Ed.

[26] Robbins, Stever. "Exit Strategies for Your Business." *Entrepreneur*. Entrepreneur Media, Inc., 26 June 2005. Web. 25 Feb. 2017.

[27] Schneider, Marc. "Moog Music Being Sold to Employees." *Billboard*. Billboard-Hollywood Reporter Media Group, 11 June 2015. Web. 26 Feb. 2017.

[28] Schneider, *Ibid*.

[29] Robbins, Stever. "Exit Strategies for Your Business." *Entrepreneur.* Entrepreneur Media, Inc., 26 June 2005. Web. 25 Feb. 2017.

[30] Dan Charnas, *The Big Payback: The History of the Business of Hip-Hop.* (New York: New American Library/Penguin Group, 2010), 573–574

[31] Charnas, *Ibid.* 575–576

[32] Robbins, Stever. "Exit Strategies for Your Business." *Entrepreneur.* Entrepreneur Media, Inc., 26 June 2005. Web. 25 Feb. 2017.

[33] Robbins, *Ibid.*

[34] "REAL HIP-HOP NETWORK, INC (Form: S-1)." *Nasdaq.* Nasdaq, Inc., 27 Aug. 2013. Web. 27 Feb. 2017.

ABOUT THE AUTHOR

Giles Miller grew up in a respectable suburban household with a successful, 125-year-old family business in manufacturing doing traditional lower-upper class activities like running, swimming, golf, croquet, polo, and falconry. At the same time that he was sunning himself at the country club in the 1980's and 90's, rap music was taking off. He didn't know it at the time, but the hip hop artists and music to which he was listening would one day reveal their secrets to teach them valuable lessons about successfully leading a $140 million dollar family business, Phoenix Closures, the largest privately held bottle cap manufacturer in America.

Giles' long path in leadership started when he graduated from Boston College and entered the US Air Force. In his 15-year career he served in the wars on the air and the ground with four tours in Iraq and Afghanistan and additional service in Italy, Germany, Hungary, Poland, Ukraine, and Korea. Giles is a graduate of the

US Air Force's Squadron Officer School and Air Command and Staff College. He is fluent in English, Spanish, and Italian, and he has a M.B.A from Oklahoma City University.

As Co-President of Phoenix Closures he presided over a 40% increase in topline revenue and a similar expansion in total production assisting in the site selection and construction of a new state of the art manufacturing facility.

Giles is the family's lone musician and is currently experimenting with bagpipes in hip-hop.

He lives in Chicago. His place is totally baller, and he is actively trying to revive the show *Cribs* just to have his home featured . . .

CPSIA information can be obtained
at www.ICGtesting.com
Printed in the USA
FFOW03n0213030118
44259672-43785FF